Forty Ways To Say Thank You, Lord

James R. Bjorge

AUGSBURG Publishing House • Minneapolis

This book is dedicated to the people and pastors of my home congregation, American Lutheran Church of Windom, Minnesota. It was in that congregational nest that I was nourished as a fledgling and encouraged to try my spiritual wings. It has been an exciting flight!

FORTY WAYS TO SAY THANK YOU, LORD

Copyright © 1981 Augsburg Publishing House
Library of Congress Catalog Card No. 80-67802
International Standard Book No. 0-8066-1864-7

Scripture quotations unless otherwise noted are from the Revised Standard Version of the Bible, copyright 1946, 1952, and 1971 by the Division of Christian Education of the National Council of Churches.

MANUFACTURED IN THE UNITED STATES OF AMERICA

Contents

Preface

God is not a lonely soul who needs your thanks or mine in order to keep his composure and continue his gracious works on planet Earth. But he is deserving of our gratitude. And we need to say thank you in order that we might retain a proper perspective and balance, a sense of values in this world in which we live.

Early in the summer of 1979 I was preparing this manuscript for publication. It was a serene time and the sunshine was in full bloom those days. But storm clouds which were hid from my view were gathering on the horizon as I sat at my desk typing out words of thanksgiving. The tempest hit one night when my son and some friends were playing in our garage and a neighbor boy was accidentally shot. The days dragged by in the humid and oppressive air of uncertainty. Recovery did come, but slowly. The sun did break through the clouds.

The summer moved on. Because of the shooting incident our planned week's vacation with my mother at the lake was postponed until the middle of July. The days we spent along the shore of Lake Carlos at Alexandria, Minnesota, were filled with family fun. Mom was her usual optimistic self even though still suffering from a stroke which had partially paralyzed her a year and a half before. Her spirits soared with talk and laughter during those days at the lake.

On Saturday afternoon I brought Mom back home to Windom where she was residing in a nursing home. That night I went to sleep at the old family house which was filled with nostalgic memories of childhood and growing teenage years. The house was up for sale but at that time it had not yet been sold. I lay awake for some time that evening as my mind was a stage for remembrances to dance across. I felt warm and good inside. It seemed as though I had just dozed off when I was awakened by the ring of the doorbell. I jumped up, pulled on my pants, and, as I arrived at the front door, was confronted by a policeman. He said that my mother had been taken to the hospital. I sensed that another stroke had made a capricious attack. When I rushed into the hospital room, my suspicions were confirmed. Mom had already lost all her speech ability and was sinking into a coma. Five days later she died.

Mother was always a source of inspiration to her three sons. Her Christian style wore well in the presence of family and friends. As we stood silently by the grave it seemed as though the door of heaven was left slightly ajar and the breeze of eternity gently blew over us. It assured us of God's love and grace until our time for the good journey would come.

Now Mom's memory continues to uplift and encourage me. I agree with the ancient sage of Scripture: "The memory of the righteous is a blessing" (Prov. 10:7). After the tears dried I was given a song in my spirit for a mother who waits for her three sons on God's heavenly shore. And how thankful I am for the days together at the lake before her departure. My two brothers were also there at that time. What a launching pad that was for her trip to eternity!

There is an old proverb: "All sunshine and no rain make a desert." Well, there was rain in the summer of 1979 in the Bjorge family. But the rain of sorrow enabled some new growth and fresh hope. In the soil of grief the seeds of gratitude found a suitable condition in which to germinate. I am convinced that 40 ways to say thank you to God is only a small beginning. Let us continue to discover ways to thank him for the boundless blessings of his grace.

SAY IT FOR . . .

Always and for everything *giving thanks in the name of our Lord Jesus Christ to God the Father.*
EPHESIANS 5:20

When one of my children said his nighttime prayers, he would list every conceivable thing on his verbal chain of thanksgiving. Bugs, birds, bees, and boats were all brought before the presence of God. And that was quite all right. I'm glad that there is a heavenly Father to whom we can address our thanks for little boys and blue skies.

Martin Luther makes an impressive list of the Father's generous givings in the meaning to the first article of the Apostles' Creed. He sums it up by stating: "Therefore I surely ought to thank and praise, serve and obey him."

1 | Say it for creation

*Make a joyful noise to God, all the
earth; sing the glory of his name;
give to him glorious praise! . . . All
the earth worships thee; they sing
praises to thee.* (Ps. 66:1-2, 4)

Creation was crafted by the mind
and will of God, and it is good. Consequently, if I
truly love and thank God, I will also love his creation. A line in Keat's "Ode to a Nightingale" says
"I cannot see what flowers are at my feet." Now that
is a shame. To fail to be alive to the bountiful beauty
of water, sky, and green grass is to fail in our love
of God. Robert Louis Stevenson once prayed that
the Celestial Surgeon would stab his spirit awake to
his books, his food, and summer rain.

Once a Puritan was walking with a friend through
the forest. As the friend stopped to admire a lovely
wild flower, the Puritan said, "I have learned to call
nothing lovely in this lost and sinful world." I don't
know where he learned that, but I do know it was
not from Scripture. The doctrine of creation makes

the world we live in God's world. His fingerprints are left on the flowers of the field and the sands of the sea. Alfred Tennyson (1809-1892) bathed in the mystery of it. He wrote:

> Flower in the crannied wall,
> I pluck you out of the crannies,
> I hold you here, root and all, in my hand,
> Little flower—but if I could understand
> What you are, root and all, and all in all,
> I should know what God and man is.

Jesus was very much aware of God's good creation. He spoke tenderly of the lilies of the field and the birds of the air. He was alive to the sower going out to sow. He ate the grain of the field with thanksgiving to God and increased the wine at the wedding in Cana. His roots clung to the earth even though he came from God and was going back to God.

When I take time to pause and ponder at the magnificent holdings in my Father's household of creation, I am, in a real sense, showing gratitude to the owner who shares it all with me. My shoes of business must frequently be set aside as I slip into my slippers and silently walk into the woods and see God at work. Elizabeth Barrett Browning captured this expectant mood in her verse:

> Earth's crammed with heaven,
> And every common bush afire with God.
> But only he who sees takes off his shoes—
> The rest sit around it and pluck blackberries.

My mother, after suffering a stroke, was in a nursing home. One day I was repotting some plants for her that she kept in her window. In the process I spilled some dirt on the table, and Mom proceeded to scoop it up in her hand. I quickly told her I would do it. She responded, "Jim, I like the feel of garden dirt. I don't get to touch it much anymore." Beautiful! Mom always loved creation, and her gardens were testimony to it. Dietrich Bonhoeffer said, "The earth which nourishes me has a rightful claim on my work and energy in return. I have no right to despise the earth on which I live and move. I am bound to it by loyalty and gratitude. . . . It would be evading his call if I were to dream away my earthly life in longing thoughts of heaven." We are all invited to enjoy the earth upon which we walk.

Gratitude grows in garden rows.

2 | Say it for salvation

Thanks be to God for his inexpressible gift! (2 Cor. 9:15).

Paul's life, following his conversion experience, could be wrapped up in one word —response. His wanderings and his writings were expressions of gratitude for God's salvation revealed to him in Jesus Christ.

It was summertime, and a group of young people from our church were spending a week at camp in the Black Hills. One afternoon they traveled to nearby Sylvan Lake to spend some time swimming in the cool, clear waters. A large rock formation a short distance from the shoreline beckoned the adventuresome. They climbed its ledges and jubilantly jumped and dived into the blue waters below.

As the time slipped by, one by one they swam back to shore after experiencing the thrills which the towering rock and the refreshing water supplied. All of a sudden a boy began to thrash in the water as he was heading for the shoreline. He was a poor swimmer and never should have attempted going to the diving rock at all. As he hollered, he swallowed water and began to panic. One of his buddies a few yards behind him came to his rescue. His friend knew the lifesaving procedures and promptly got him to shore.

Later, in the dressing room of the bathhouse, the fellows were combing their hair and getting ready to go back to camp. The rescuer reached into his pocket for his comb only to find he had forgotten it. He then asked the young man whom he had pulled from the water for his comb. The answer was quick, "I don't want to get your dandruff on my comb!" Then there was a silent pause. He knew at once the stupidity of his statement. He had just denied the use of his cheap comb to a fellow who had just saved his life. He handed over his comb, a sheepish grin covering his embarrassment.

Aesop told a fable of the slave Androcles who escaped from his master and fled into the forest. There he came upon a lion groaning in pain. At first he turned to flee, but when the lion did not follow, he went back and found that the lion's paw was swollen and bleeding from a huge thorn. He pulled out the thorn and remained with the lion, sheltered by him in his den. Shortly afterward both Androcles and the lion were captured. The slave was sentenced to be thrown to the lions in the royal amphitheater for the amusement of the emperor. When the lion was unleashed, he rushed toward his victim. On closer examination, however, he recognized the man as his friend Androcles. Instead of devouring the slave, the lion licked his hands like a friendly dog. When the surprised emperor learned the story from Androcles, he released both the slave and the lion.

The story is a familiar one, but perhaps not so well known are the words which Aesop added to the fable. "Gratitude is the sign of noble souls." When I think of God's great rescue mission at Calvary, saving me from sin, death, and the power of the devil, how can I say no if he asks for my comb of courtesy to others or my tools for the teaching of his love?

The rendition of gratitude is a responsive chord.

3 | Say it for guidance

Trust in the Lord with all your heart, and do not rely on your own insight. In all your ways acknowledge him, and he will make straight your paths (Prov. 3:5-6).

He leads me . . . (Ps. 23:2b).

Meaningless is one of the great plagues that muddle up the mind of man. As Macbeth said, "Life is full of sound and fury and signifies nothing." There is so much motion in our day and there seems to be so little direction. We go round and round and get nowhere fast. Is there nothing on which to stay our minds so we may be stayed?

Have you ever been lost while driving? Most people have experienced this dilemma at one time or another. The solution is not to aimlessly drive, looking for some familiar signpost to lead you out of your lostness; rather, you need to stop and ask for guidance from someone familiar with the area. After receiving directions it becomes relatively easy to get your bearing and be on your way to your destination.

God offers such assistance to all earthly pilgrims who are on the move. His directions will never lead you down a blind alley, nor will you ever end up on a dead-end street. With his assistance you will not only arrive at your destination but you will enjoy the process of getting there.

When I was a small boy, I used to collect butterflies. My favorite was the monarch with its beautiful black veining and its elegant, orange-tinted wings. Until recently the migration of the monarch was a complete mystery. Now it has been discovered that the monarch butterfly, which weighs only as much as a paper clip, flies all the way to Mexico for the winter season. There, in a few remote high-altitude sanctuaries, the monarch rests until spring arrives. The temperature in those regions is perfect for the partial hibernation of the monarch, ranging from 42 to 60 degrees Fahrenheit—too warm to freeze and too cold to do much flying.

Now here is the miracle of it all. When the milkweed plant, upon which the monarch feeds, is lush and ripe in Texas, the monarch starts the northward flight. It lays eggs on the Texas milkweed. A caterpillar emerges after three to twelve days. The caterpillar, with its huge appetite, eats, sheds its skin several times, and then forms a chrysalis. Two weeks later, the adult butterfly emerges from the casket of the cocoon. Three days after leaving the chrysalis, the adult butterfly is ready to mate and begin a new generation.

The monarch that migrated from Minnesota to Mexico, and then in the spring mated and began a new generation in Texas, will die en route on the northern flight. The children will feed on milkweeds as they continue on the northward trek and will arrive in Minnesota in late May or early June. These monarchs will mate and live out a brief six-week lifetime. The grandchildren of the Mexican monarchs will be born in Minnesota, and they will mate in late August or early September. Then in this generation something peculiar happens. The reproductive chemistry and life processes are slowed down, permitting these monarchs to live seven months rather than six weeks. Thus they are enabled to make the 2000 mile flight to Mexico for the winter season.

How can a butterfly, buffeted by blustery winds and pelted by rain, make its way over unfamiliar terrain? How can this butterfly, at least three generations removed from those that made last year's flight, fly over city and countryside to find a secluded hideaway in Mexico? It is an awesome thing! Only God, who created the little creature, knows the secret.

Will not this same God care for me if I stop and ask him for directions? I am sure he will. All I can say is, "Thanks, Lord." Now I can travel with confidence. "I took courage, for the hand of the Lord my God was upon me" (Ezra 7:28b).

I will be filled with gratitude to God for guidance.

17

4 | Say it for memory

The memory of the righteous is a blessing (Prov. 10:7).

They remembered that God was their rock, the Most High God their redeemer (Ps. 78:35).

The memory is a great channel or antenna of human reception that picks up the waves of God's goodness and human kindness. Today we are prone to emphasize the spirit of forging ahead, looking for future blessings, health, and happiness. In our straining to collect something new we have failed to spend much time in recollecting. The chamber of memory in our minds gets dusty, and the furniture of past blessings fades from the conscious mind.

I need to clean house in the chamber of memory. In so doing I discover anew some rare pieces of God's providence and uncover some forgotten gifts from friends. I learn from the cattle of the field the value of chewing my mental cud in meditation. Then I have opportunity to digest what has been speedily devoured in the days of life. The old suggestion given in a hymn has much merit, "Count your many blessings, name them one by one, and it will surprise you what the Lord hath done."

The mind travels back over the times of childhood, and we think of our parents. We remember their sleepless nights, their sacrifices and their anxieties, as they followed us through our growing pains. They held us in love and at the same time gently nudged us from the nest hoping we would learn to fly on our own. We recall the friends who went to bat for us when we would have lost the game without their help. We remember the old schoolhouse where teachers took some great pains in planting seeds in stubborn minds.

The memory not only stirs up the tendernesses and goodnesses of the past but also fortifies us for the future. Memory can prevent us from making the same mistakes twice. Henrik Ibsen, the Norwegian author, tells of a rector who was often tempted to do evil. Each time, at the point of yielding, he looked at the portraits of his godly ancestors which hung on the wall in his home. Each seemed to speak a word which held him back. A saving and guarding power in the memory waits to be tapped.

Henry Nelson Wieman once suggested that, just as the devout Roman Catholic has a string of beads called a rosary to keep track of his prayers, so each of us needs a mental rosary to keep track of our beads of blessing. When we sit down with the saints and begin to comprehend the love of God in Christ Jesus, its breadth and length and height and depth, something begins to well up in the heart, and we cannot keep it from overflowing. As we kneel at the altar to receive the sacrament with the words, "Do this in remembrance of me," the mind starts to mirror the mighty acts of God's deliverance in world history and in our personal story.

As James Barrie said, "God has given us memories that we might have roses in December."

The roots of remembrance give rise to the sweet grapes of gratitude.

5 | Say it for forgiveness

Who is a God like thee, pardoning iniquity and passing over transgression for the remnant of his inheritance? He does not retain his anger for ever because he delights in steadfast love (Mic. 7:18).

It happened in this way. A man was leaning against the wall of his house as the gentle afternoon breezes cooled the perspiration on his face. He was relaxed as his mind shifted into neutral, and his eyes slowly surveyed the surrounding scenery. A door slammed, startling him. He straightened up and peered over the fence where the neighbor lady had just stepped out of the house. She stood there in a long, loose robe which billowed against the configuration of her body. She had but one garment upon her. There on the deck was a large basin of water. She slowly walked toward it with the litheness of a cat. She reached up and unfastened a brooch at her neck. The white linen gown fluttered down like an autumn leaf, leaving her naked against the cool blue sky.

The man's heart skipped a beat as she unashamedly began to wash herself. She bent over the basin, cupped some water in her hands, and let it trickle over her throat, shoulders, and ample breasts. It was not long until her whole body was wet and luminous. Soon a towel was caressing her body as she drew it from side to side with the movement of undulating waves. Desire swelled as the man drank in the ripeness of this body set free in the dancing sunbeams. As she leaned over to gather up her robe, he turned to retreat into the house only to strike his foot noisily against a small table. The woman looked over, and their glances met. He expected her to cry out, but her lips never moved. However, he noticed the corners of her mouth indented by a slight indolent smile. He knew she had not minded his viewing as she drew the robe around her and departed from sight.

The man could not forget her. Thoughts of desire stirred inside him as his mind brooded over her opulent breasts and her body yielding to his touch. He just had to invite her over. That was the start of a series of troubles. The man was King David, and the woman was Bathsheba. Adultery was the result. This was compounded by murder as David, in an attempt to cover his sin, sent her husband Uriah into the front lines of war and ordered the other soldiers to retreat so Uriah would be killed.

David began to wilt under the weight of guilt. His "strength was dried up as by the heat of summer" (Ps. 32:4). Could God ever forgive such a flagrant violation of his laws? David had stolen another man's wife and then was also responsible for that man's death. David cried out to God in his misery. In his prayer of distress also comes the answer to his plight: "Blessed is he whose transgression is forgiven, whose sin is covered. Blessed is the man to whom the Lord imputes no iniquity" (Ps. 32:1-2). In repentance David found release as God, in his grace, restored their relationship.

A Buddhist priest was asked, "What do you think the Christian religion has to offer which the Buddhist religion does not have?" The reply was simply, "The forgiveness of sins." That forgiveness, although it cost God so much, is free to us. If forgiveness for your failings does not set your heart to singing songs of thanksgiving, nothing will! "In him we have redemption through his blood, the forgiveness of our trespasses, according to the riches of his grace which he lavished upon us" (Eph. 1:7-8).

Forgiving grace is the foundation of gratitude.

6 | Say it for example

Be imitators of me, as I am of Christ (1 Cor. 11:1).

Therefore be imitators of God, as beloved children (Eph. 5:1).

A small boy had a cage full of sparrows. He thought they should be able to learn to sing like canaries. He therefore purchased a canary and put it in the cage with them. "Teach them to sing," he ordered the yellow songster. A few days later the boy ran to his mother with the news, "Mom, the canary is chirping like the sparrows!"

A Dutch proverb warns, "He who lives with cripples will learn to limp." The New Testament verse advises us, "Bad company ruins good morals" (1 Cor. 15:33). On the other hand, while bad company can be a disuasion, good company can be an inspiration. While bad company can be a deterrent to good behavior, good company can be a propellent. Another old proverb says, "Live with a singer if you would learn to sing."

My father once said about Jesus, "There was my

perfect hero. Men are only little boys grown a little bigger, especially around the middle. I am now a man but still I am a hero worshipper, and Jesus is my hero." To be sure, Jesus was more than a hero to my father. He was also his Savior. The hero aspect was of great importance, though, for Dad sought to imitate Jesus as Paul exhorted his readers to do. This association with Jesus rubbed off on Dad, and everyone could perceive that he had spent time with his Lord.

In the realm of gratitude Jesus is the pacesetter for all of us. If I were an artist, I would paint three pictures of Jesus and hang them on the walls of your daily living. The first picture would show 5000 people milling around in a meadow. Jesus has just finished speaking about the kingdom of God at an outdoor rally. He is concerned about all the needs of the people, and at this time the most immediate need is for food—the people are hungry. Andrew places in his hands the lunch of a little lad, but what is this when the multitude is so many? Most people would have complained about having so little when so much was needed. Jesus, however, took the lunch, looked up to heaven, and blessed the loaves and fishes. He gave thanks!

The next picture would frame Jesus at a table with 12 men. The time for him to climb the hill of Calvary is close at hand. In human terms it seemed as though everything would be lost; nothing gained. Yet even at this time, he took bread in his hands, "and when he had given thanks, he broke it and gave it to them, saying, 'This is my body which is given for you' "

(Luke 22:19). Instead of complaining about his predicament he shared with them a meal of thanksgiving.

The third picture would show Jesus with a group of people gathered at the grave of Lazarus. When Lazarus died, Jesus wept. The old Jewish saying was being enacted, "For every tear on earth that flows, God the ruler surely knows." Jesus confronted the situation with confidence and not with criticism. Before raising Lazarus Jesus lifted up his eyes and said, "Father, I thank thee that thou hast heard me" (John 11:41). Gratitude at the grave was a unique example.

Someone said, "The best way to send an idea is to wrap it up in a person." Gratitude was always conveyed in the life of Christ. Therefore, look to Jesus and be like him. Your friends will see his likeness in the things you say and do each day.

Gratitude is caught as well as taught.

7 | Say it for today

This is the day which the Lord has made; let us rejoice and be glad in it (Ps. 118:24).

There is an old tale about a gambler who rubbed Aladdin's lamp and was confronted by a genie who told him he could have one wish. He pondered the gracious offer for a few moments and then made his pronouncement: "I wish to have tomorrow's newspaper." The wish was quickly granted, and with greedy delight the gambler turned to the sheet which held the racing results. Now he could hurry to the track and place his bets on sure winners. A smirk of satisfaction crossed his face as he paged through the rest of the paper. The smile turned into a frown as his eyes glanced at the obituary column. Heading the list of names was his own. All his anticipated gains would now be gone with the visit of the grim reaper.

Some people spend too much time on the street corner looking into yesterdays. They grieve over past mistakes and gloat over past successes. Neither is healthy. The greatest thing we can do with our yesterdays is to place them into God's hands, and because of his forgiving grace we can forget the bad and thank him for the good.

Our tomorrows are future gifts. We must not try to open these packages in advance. It is good to dream and plan wisely for tomorrow, but we can't live on that street today. Worrying about the future will only sap our strength for today. Jesus said, "Therefore do not be anxious about tomorrow, for tomorrow will be anxious for itself. Let the day's own trouble be sufficient for the day" (Matt. 6:34). He taught us to pray, "Give us this day our daily bread."

Moses gave the following promise to the tribe of Asher, "And as your days, so shall your strength be" (Deut. 33:25). When God supplied manna in a miraculous fashion to the Israelites in the wilderness, they were not allowed to store it for a rainy day. If they hoarded it, the manna would spoil. It had to be gathered fresh every morning. In the same way he imparts his grace—a new supply to each of us every day.

Dr. Alvin Rogness pointed up the preciousness of today when he said, "There is no time for rehearsal. The great play is on. Every day is another block of time in which to live—to live, to love, to serve, to weep, and to laugh. You cannot employ today only to set the stage for tomorrow. There may be no tomorrow." There is wisdom wrapped in that statement! I can get so caught up in the destination of tomorrow that I forget to enjoy the trip of today.

28

Today is my opportunity to express thanks to family, friends, and my Father in heaven. Today is a gift that must be carefully unwrapped for there may be many surprises crammed in the corners and crevices of the box.

You say thank you to God when you live today to the fullest extent. Time is a rich resource which God gives you today.

> Look to this Day!
> For Yesterday is but a Dream,
> And Tomorrow is only a Vision:
> But Today well lived makes
> Every Yesterday a Dream of Happiness,
> And every Tomorrow a Vision of Hope.
> Look well therefore to this Day!
> Such is the Salutation of the Dawn!
>   Based on the Sanskrit, c. 1200 B.C.

Thanksgiving is designed for every day.

8 | Say it for labor

Whatever your task, work heartily, as serving the Lord and not men (Col. 3:23).

Thank God for your work! Many people would respond to that in the negative. They don't look upon work as a gift from God, but rather as a tedious exercise performed to put food on the table and money for play in the pocket.

Whenever I need to get my thinking in the proper perspective for thanking God for work, I go back and reread the creation account. "Thus the heavens and the earth were finished, and all the host of them. And on the seventh day God finished his work which he had done, and he rested on the seventh day from all his work which he had done" (Gen. 2:1-2). God wore his overalls when he toiled over this earth, shaping it and filling it with many good things. God has not been standing in an unemployment line since that time either, nor is he about to retire. God keeps right on creating and renewing. That is his nature.

You and I were created in the image of this great God. Does it then seem reasonable that we should find satisfaction in loafing and killing time? Of course not. After each of God's creative acts he stepped back, and the Scripture account says, "And God saw that it was good." When we labor creatively and do good work, the result is a good feeling. Why? Simply because we are living out this image of God within us.

The writer of Proverbs gets a little irritated by the sluggishness of many people. He exhorts them: "Go to the ant, O sluggard; consider her ways and be wise" (Prov. 6:6). An ant colony is a busy place with every member of the colony at work. Industriousness is the way of prudence. Idleness breeds problems, and so it is that the ancient writer employs the ant to teach a lesson. The writers of Scripture have scant patience with the man who loafs his way through life and doesn't lift a finger unless he has to. Paul stitched tents and pondered over manuscripts seeking to articulate the gospel. He knew the smell of sweat. He came down hard on the folk who ran from work, "If any one will not work, let him not eat" (2 Thess. 3:10).

A man was looking for a particular piece of lumber at the yards when he noticed a man dressed in coveralls. He asked him, "Do you work here?" The reply was short: "Only if I have to." Robert Gibbings in *Lovely Is the Lee* tells of an old man with two lazy sons. Before he died, he told them there was a crock of gold buried in one of his fields not more than 18 inches beneath the surface. When the old man was gone, the sons began to dig furiously. They dug in deep furrows over every inch of the fields for fear of missing it. They never found it. Then they decided that they might as well plant the fields with oats since they were dug up. The money they made from their oats was worth more than any crock of gold. Inadvertently they learned the lesson of work which their father had ingeniously intended.

As you begin thanking God for your daily work, your attitude also begins to be transformed. You sense the presence of the divine companion who once worked in a carpenter's shop. You understand that those who work without complaining do the holy will of God. In our prayer of thanksgiving for work we request his help to do our best and lead us to our Sabbath rest.

Toil that binds mankind together is cause for thanksgiving.

9 | Say it for God's invitations

Put on then, as God's chosen ones, holy and beloved, compassion, kindness, lowliness, meekness, and patience, forbearing one another and, if one has a complaint against another, forgiving each other; as the Lord has forgiven you, so you also must forgive. And above all these put on love (Col. 3:12-14).

Suppose you have two daughters, and you want to surprise them with new summer attire. You take great pains in the proper selection of the latest fashions which teenagers are now purchasing. Both daughters express excitement as they stumble upon these new clothes which you secretly hung in their respective closets. Both daughters thank you profusely for your parental gifts. However, as the days pass by only one of your daughters is wearing her new apparel. So you ask the other if she does not like what you selected for her. She replies, "Oh, thank you very much for the clothes. I'm merely saving them for later on." First of all, this will teach you quickly what all parents learn sooner or later—that teenagers like to pick out their own clothes. The second fact revealed is that thanks is shown in the wearing and not merely by verbal expression.

God has supplied for us a wardrobe that is appropriate for all seasons. It will look good and wear well on everybody. The timeless style is stitched by the hand of God. He invites you to drop by his store and try it on. The price of the new wardrobe is free. At this point the gratitude to God comes not from the admiration of the clothes but from the wearing of them. And his wardrobe consists of compassion, kindness, patience, and love.

Let's use another analogy. A man walks into a restaurant, sits down, and accepts a menu from the waitress. As she returns for his order, he exclaims, "I like the cover on the menu, but I think the format could be improved." He then makes suggestions for prices and artistic arrangements on the menu. The waitress gets impatient and asks him to please place his order. The customer gives her a puzzled look and says, "Oh, I'm not really interested in eating. I'm a connoisseur of menus."

Some people make a habit of conversing about religion over the coffee cup. They may have a fine collection of the various translations of the Bible. They may have minored in religion during college days. But until they accept the invitation to participate in the banquet, they are merely fooling around with the menu.

"The Spirit and the Bride say, 'Come.' And let him

who hears say, 'Come.' And let him who is thirsty come, let him who desires take the water of life without price" (Rev. 22:17). Jesus invites us to the banquet of the Lord's table and urges us to "do this in remembrance of me." The invitation comes each Sunday to gather with the communion of saints into a fellowship of praise to seek his will and be equipped to lead a Christian life.

A rejection, no matter how nicely it is phrased, is a "No thanks" to God when he offers us his wardrobe to wear and his banquet to attend and his goodness to experience. The proof of gratitude comes in the wearing and the eating.

An invitation accepted is gratitude expressed.

10 Say it for struggle

> *Brethren, I do not consider that I have made it my own; but one thing I do, forgetting what lies behind and straining forward to what lies ahead, I press on toward the goal for the prize of the upward call of God in Christ Jesus* (Phil. 3:13-14).

A certain amateur naturalist was observing an emperor moth slowly and laboriously going through the chrysalis stage. Day by day there seemed to be a squirming and a striving going on in the casket of the cocoon. It seemed so painful a way to be born. This compassionate man then decided to help the birth process by slitting the cocoon with his pen knife, making it easier for the moth to emerge. This he did, and this cocoon cesarean caused a premature birth. The struggle was over for the new moth, but the moth was born frail and feeble, unable to cope with its new environment.

By misappropriated kindness the amateur naturalist

had become an enemy of the moth. Unwittingly he had deprived the moth of the strength that comes only by struggle. Life is that way for all creatures. Struggle seems to put color in the cheeks, light in the eyes, and confidence in the soul. There are no short-cuts to great achievements. Worthwhile contributions to life always seem to arrive through the gateway of courageous challenge.

A little boy was looking at a geography book and exclaimed to his mother, "Why are the rivers crooked?" The answer is really quite simple. The rivers follow the paths of least resistance, skirting the boulders and hard places and winding through the shifting sand. I must admit that human lives seem to get crooked in the same fashion. When we skirt struggles as we avoid puddles, we rob ourselves of the growth that comes through the disciplined exercise of physical, moral, and mental muscles.

The Apostle Paul uses the expression of "straining forward" to characterize the seriousness of the Christian race. Chesterton once said, "Christianity has not been tried and found wanting; it has been found hard and not tried."

It is said the north wind made the Vikings. I am sure that wind helped as they developed tenacity of character battling the elements. Arnold Toynbee, the historian, said, "It is difficulties and obstacles that lead to the flowering of any civilization." Perhaps that is also true of individuals. Don Schollander, an Olympic champion in the Tokyo games of 1964, said, "The most important thing in the Olympic Games is not to win but to take part, just as the most important thing in life is not the triumph but the struggle. The essential thing is . . . to have fought well."

In Christ we become "more than conquerors" as we face our struggles in the service of our Lord and his people. I, for one, would not prefer to be carried to the skies on flowery beds of ease, but rather struggle with those who sail on stormy seas. Struggle seems to be the seed that sends forth new growth. For that I thank God!

Thanks for storms that I have weathered.

SAY IT WITH . . .

Praise him with trumpet sound;
praise him with lute and harp!
Praise him with timbrel and dance;
praise him with strings and pipe!
Praise him with sounding cymbals;
praise him with loud clashing cymbals!
Let everything that breathes
praise the Lord!

PSALM 150:3-6

The musician says, "Say it with music!"
The florist will comment, "Say it with flowers!" The
manufacturer of rich chocolates will advertise, "Say
it with candy!" There are many ways to express
thoughtfulness and thankfulness to those whom we
love. There are equally as many ways of thanking and
praising God.

And remember, as we say it "to one of the least
of these," Jesus wants us to know that we are saying
it to him. Various vessels carry the cargo of gratitude.

11 | Say it with smiles

A glad heart makes a cheerful countenance (Prov. 15:13).

The Lord gave to Moses a beautiful benediction with which to bless Israel, "The Lord bless you and keep you: The Lord make his face to shine upon you, and be gracious to you: The Lord lift up his countenance upon you, and give you peace" (Num. 6:24-26). God knew how to smile!

What sunshine is to flowers, smiles are to humanity. I remember back in high school days there was a beautiful brunette who was in the grade above me. She walked with the grace of a gazelle catching the roving eyes of the boys. Brains and beauty were superbly gathered together in this young woman. But a special gift she gave was a smile that spilled over on all those in her company. In the school yearbook the following words were printed under her picture: The most eloquent lines aren't spoken; they are worn.

A grateful heart wrapped in a thankful smile is a gift of great value. A smile gives a lift to the weary and gladdens the sad. Donny and Marie Osmond of the singing Osmond family once stated that each of the children has a responsibility in its family life. In the interview Donny grinned and said that he and Marie were "in charge of smiling."

Grace is a face, the face of Christ and of Christian acceptance. Jesus was "full of grace and truth" (John 1:14). That which was on the inside surfaced on his face so that people of all ages drew near to him and felt comfortable and at ease. Frank, open faces speak a nonverbal invitation to fellowship.

A story is told about President Jefferson and a group of companions who were riding horseback cross-country and were obliged to ford a swollen stream. A wayfarer waited until several of the party had crossed and then hailed President Jefferson, asking to be ferried across. The president took him up on the back of the horse and later set him down on the opposite bank. "Tell me," asked one of the men, "why did you select the president for this favor?" The man answered, "I didn't know he was the president. All I know is that on some of the faces was written the answer no and on some of them the answer yes. His was a yes face."

Don't be stingy with your smiles. The more you give away the more you will have. If you did not begin this day with a smile, why not start practicing for tomorrow?

A thank you and a smile are partners.

12 | Say it with deeds

*If a brother or a sister is ill-clad
and in lack of daily food, and one
of you says to them, "Go in peace,
be warmed and filled," without
giving them the things needed for
the body, what does it profit?*
(James 2:15-16).

William Jennings Bryan once remarked that he had learned that not everyone who applauds for you will vote for you. Words are quite cheap in the marketplace of life; deeds have a cost attached to them. However, when the appropriate words are attached to the action of doing, you have a compelling combination.

The phrase "Big talk, little do," is not the way of thanksliving. I am increasingly convinced that real love involves little conversation and a lot of action. It consumes large chunks of time and expenditure of energy. The world cries today for a "show me" love. Principles enunciated and hopes expressed will not do the job without the concrete expression of caring and compassion. John Drinkwater said, "Give us to build above the deep intent, the deed, the deed." Dag Hammerskjöld was quoted saying, "The road to holiness necessarily passes through action." So does the road of thanksgiving.

The amazing thing that happens every time you do a deed of love toward a fellow person is that it rebounds right into the presence of God. When one of my children receives a gift, a job, or a compliment, I will respond with, "Thank you." Why? Because we belong to the same family and all the family is blessed when one of its members is rewarded. My heavenly Father feels the same way every time one of his earthlings is energized by an act of kindness. Paul talks about generous living to the church at Corinth, "For the rendering of this service not only supplies the wants of the saints but also overflows in many thanksgivings to God" (2 Cor. 9:12).

Some years ago on a cold October morning a newspaper boy in the big city was out on the job selling his papers. He was standing barefoot, warming his feet on a grating below which was a bakery. A pastor's wife came along and saw how he was shivering in the cold. She asked him whether he had any shoes, and his reply was negative. She then asked him if he would like some. Indeed, he surely would. She took him to a department store and purchased him some socks and shoes. The young lad immediately ran out of the store and resumed selling his papers. He did not even take time to say thanks. The pastor's wife was somewhat disappointed with his ingratitude. As she was leaving the store, the little fellow came back in and asked, "Lady, I wanta ask you a question. Are you God's wife?" She was taken aback and began to stutter, "Why—ah—no, but I am one of his children." The boy quickly responded, "Well, I knowed you must be some kin of his."

Do you want to say thank you to God this day? Then open your front door and go out to a neighbor with a deed tucked under your arm. The thrust will be twofold as thanks bounces from earth to heaven.

The creed of gratitude is affirmed in deed.

13 | Say it with generosity

We want you to know, brethren, about the grace of God which has been shown in the churches of Macedonia, for in a severe test of affliction, their abundance of joy and their extreme poverty have overflowed in a wealth of liberality on their part. For they gave according to their means, as I can testify, and beyond their means, of their own free will, begging us earnestly for the favor of taking part in the relief of the saints (2 Cor. 8:1-4).

What a magnificent statement of generosity. Note the expressions: "abundance of joy," "overflowed in a wealth of liberality," "beyond their means." True gratitude always grows into self-forgetful generosity.

As David speaks of God's tender care for the sheep, he uses the words, "my cup overflows." God is never stingy! When Jesus fed the 5000, there were baskets of bounty left over. I have always admired the first Palm Sunday crowd. The people were carried outside of themselves by the power of a great emotion. Such surging hope prevailed that day that they threw their good coats on the dust and mud of the road. Their garments were spoiled in this spontaneous display of overflowing excitement.

Remember the poor woman at the temple? Love was generating her spirit, and she threw her last two coins into the church coffers. Jesus praised her for her generosity. Another woman anointed Jesus with a box of very precious perfume. Some of the disciples were indignant over the waste, arguing that it might have been sold and the money given to the poor. We can hear them say, "Go easy on that stuff, sister. It costs good money in these days of inflation." But Jesus had been waiting for this kind of reckless display of thanksgiving to God. He said, "Wherever the gospel is preached in the whole world, what she has done will be told in memory of her" (Mark 14:9).

When thanksgiving lifts you out of yourself in self-forgetfulness, it is great faith in action. You are truly saying thanks to God when you give to the church generously and not niggardly.

Aesop tells of a wolf who had been gorging on an animal which he had killed. A bone became stuck in his throat. He groaned and moaned for help. A crane came along and agreed to help. "I will give you anything if you will take it out," cried the wolf. The crane put his long neck down the wolf's throat and pulled out the bone. When the crane asked for his reward, the wolf grinned and showed his teeth, saying, "Be content. You have just put your head inside a wolf's mouth and taken it out in safety; that ought to be reward enough for you." At the end of the fable Aesop put these words: "Gratitude and greed go not together." Don't let greed gobble up your impulses of generosity!

The flower of gratitude becomes the fruit of generosity.

14 | Say it with letters

I, Paul, write this greeting with my own hand. . . . Grace be with you (Col. 4:18).

I was rummaging around in the attic of our house just spending a lazy afternoon doing nothing in particular. I was still in high school and my older brother, John, was away at college. Among some of his books I discovered a bundle of letters written to him by his girl friend of the preceding year. I shouldn't have opened them, but curiosity conquered my better judgement. I must admit that they provided me with some interesting reading that afternoon. A bit of guilt pricked my conscience when I thought about invading his private domain, but I quickly dismissed it with the thought that he was my brother and we should be open to one another. When he came home, I kidded him about these lovey-dovey notes. Needless to say, he was not amused by my comments nor by my nosiness.

People often keep letters tucked away in some private nook. It is not strange at all! Hearts have always yearned for the personal word of love, concern, and thanksgiving. A spoken word can be packaged and stored only in the memory. A written word is there to be read and reread. You can sit down to the banquet of a personal letter many times, and the heart will be filled and satisfied again and again. The Apostle Paul told the church at Colossae that he was writing to them with his own hand. The thanks he gave and the concern he displayed was there on paper, a constant reminder to them.

Letters can be one of the most dynamic vehicles of gratitude. Recently looking through an old scrapbook I discovered some notes written to me during school days. As I read them again, a fresh breeze brushed up against my soul, and I felt good. One came from the dean of students at St. Olaf College. He said, "Thank you very much for the fine message that you brought to us in chapel last Saturday. Your Christian witness is a source of inspiration to me and I know to others on the campus. . . ." At graduation time the athletic director at St. Olaf wrote: "Your contribution in basketball, track, and tennis has been most significant. I was so proud to have you set a new school record in the high jump on your final day of competition. Through these sports I learned to know you for the fine person you are. . . ."

When I was on seminary internship at Alexandria, Minnesota, a preaching-teaching-reaching series was conducted in the congregation. Dr. Oscar Hanson of the ALC Department of Evangelism wrote me a personal letter as he was getting ready to leave for Nor-

49

way. It contained three thank yous in the first paragraph for little things I had done during the week of meetings. It was like frosting on a cake to receive such comments from a giant in the pulpit.

Why have I saved letters like these from my younger years? Simply because they were builders of confidence. They would give the listless spirit a real lift on any day. They were documents of love from which refreshment could be drawn down through the years.

Maybe today is the right time for you to write a letter to some young fledgling who is just learning to fly. A few thank-you notes, written in a personal way, will provide blessings that will spill over into future years.

Gratitude can be spelled in many ways on a sheet of paper.

15 | Say it with compliments

*Love one another with brotherly
affection; outdo one another in
showing honor* (Rom. 12:10).

An ant climbed on an elephant's
back and asked for a ride over a bridge. The bridge
trembled under the weight of this huge beast. After
they had crossed, the ant exclaimed, "My, but didn't
we shake that bridge!" The boasting ant is a picture
of arrogance. However, we have been told so many
times about the pitfalls of bragging, boasting, and
blowing our own horns that we have also cut back
in our patting of others on the back. Paul, therefore,
exhorts us not to be stingy but rather extravagant
in showing honor to others.

Bridget, an Irish girl, attended Mass every Sunday,
and she delighted in hearing Father Murphy preach.
One Lord's day she lingered at the door of the church
and cascaded compliments on the priest for his pulpit
efforts of the day. It was quite evident that Father
Murphy was not immune to her flattery. However,
he believed that the occasion demanded a moment

of modesty so he said, "Thank you, Bridget, but let's have no more of your Irish blarney. You should know that your compliments roll off me like water from a duck's back." Bridget replied, "Maybe so, Father, but the ducks like it."

There is no question about it. All of us work best in the sunshine of approval. Have you ever noticed the many times Jesus commended people in the New Testament accounts? To be sure, Jesus did not hesitate to condemn wrongdoing. At times he humbled sinners, but he never humiliated them. He sought to bring out the best in them by showing that he expected the best from them. In the letters to the seven churches in Revelation he had some criticisms, but in all but one he first threw out commendations. It is always wise to point out that which is good before we begin to seek to eradicate that which is evil.

One Father's Day my youngest son, Benjamin, nine years old, gave me a handmade card. On it he scribbled the following words, "This is to the best Dad in the world. Happy Father's Day from Ben!" Well, to be sure, in my judgment he exaggerated a bit, but it surely made me feel good to have praise from this little caboose in the line of our five children.

Praise primes the pump for greater achievement. A well-wrapped thank you is like the song of a cardinal as it lifts your spirit and sets you soaring. Too often we are like black crows who sit on some dead branch and from the perch of such a pulpit we hurl our critical condemnations on anyone who might pass by. Crowlike calls make us want to cringe. Lives are cramped and thwarted under continual criticism. Emotions are then driven inward rather than allowed outward expression. The danger of praise "going to the head" is far less than the danger of inadequate support and disapproval.

How do you feel when someone comes up to you and says, "My, but you have fine children. They are certainly a credit to our community. I want to thank you for them."? Of course, you feel proud. A compliment to your children is also one to you. Well, how do you suppose God feels when we speak well of our fellow brothers and sisters? I think that maybe some buttons pop on his vest! God, you see, is the Father of us all.

Gratitude always encourages and never discourages.

16 | Say it with enthusiasm

And leaping up he stood and walked and entered the temple with them, walking and leaping and praising God (Acts 3:8).

That is the description of the man who was lame from birth and was healed on the steps of the temple. I like this style of letting go of himself in a reckless display of thanksgiving in the sacredness of the sanctuary.

Through the years many of us have been conditioned to serve up our gratitude in very subdued and somber ways. I am reminded of an older couple in Norway. The sailor husband returned home after a year at sea and greeted his wife at the door with a handshake. That is quite a contrast to a certain couple on a front porch. "For two cents I'd kiss you," said the young man. "Well, here's fifty cents," replied the girl.

The story of a brakeman on one of the old freight trains is a revealing one. On his very first run the train came to a steep grade which the engineer had difficulty negotiating. Upon reaching the summit, the engineer turned to his brakeman and said, "Boy, that was a hard climb, wasn't it?" The brakeman replied, "It sure was, and if I hadn't put the brake on, we would have slipped back!" Sometimes I get the feeling that the people of God often travel with their brakes on. They never let themselves go, afraid of a runaway. Whether in friendship, worship, or expression of the faith that is within, they never go on a free-for-all romp.

A little boy in our congregation delights me every Sunday. He sits with rapt attention, especially during the children's sermon. At the door he grabs my hand as if he were going to fall off a ledge. Then he begins to pump it as if he were shaking apples off an old orchard tree. That kind of enthusiasm is fun.

David exemplified thanksgiving wrapped in enthusiasm when he celebrated God's deliverance and the bringing of the Ark to Jerusalem. There was a big parade, and I am sure at least 76 trombones were in the lead. David did not stand on the sidelines watching the celebration in a state of kingly casualness. No, he was in the parade, shouting and dancing and throwing his shirt in the air. Now Michal, his wife, thought this was very undignified and disgraceful for the king. She scolded him for his lack of decency and his uninhibited display of gratitude to God. David responded, "I will make merry before the Lord" (2 Sam. 6:21).

We have quite a few people like David's wife in our churches. According to them, your emotions should always be somewhat repressed in a public place. And you should never dance before the Lord "with all your might" as David did. Therefore, when we sing praise we often do so with the volume of the voice box turned only half on. Many don't sing at all. In our attempt to preserve reverence we lose the recklessness of rejoicing with all our might.

Emerson said, "Nothing great was ever achieved without enthusiasm." Enthusiasm is the fuel for adoration and thanksgiving with which to orbit the world of God. Walt Whitman, the poet, said, "I was simmering, really simmering; Emerson brought me to a boil." Whitman, a truly gifted man, lacked power until the fire of enthusiasm brought him to the boiling point. May we all help in the glorious task of bringing our services of thanksgiving to that beautiful, bubbling, boiling point!

Gratitude should be allowed to go for broke!

17 | Say it with music

Let the word of Christ dwell in you richly, teach and admonish one another in all wisdom, and sing psalms and hymns and spiritual songs with thankfulness in your hearts to God (Col. 3:16).

Where there is celebration, that celebration always seems to be cradled in music. Music sets the mood and also motivates. Matthew and Mark state that the last act of worship in the upper room was the singing of a hymn. "And when they had sung a hymn, they went out to the Mount of Olives" (Matt. 26:30). Music was preparing Jesus for the pain of the cross. When Paul and Silas were thrown into prison, they could have cowered in a corner, but rather they courageously sang songs so all could hear. "But about midnight Paul and Silas were praying and singing hymns to God, and the prisoners were listening to them" (Acts 16:25).

Luther, in his "Discourse in Praise of Music," gives thanks to God for having bestowed the power of song on the "nightingale and the many thousand birds of the air," and again he writes, "I give music the highest and most honorable place; and everyone knows how David and all the saints put their divine thoughts into verse, rhyme, and song." Luther wrote the following emphatic statement in 1525, "If any man despises music, for him I have no liking; for music is a gift and grace of God, and not an invention of men. Thus it drives out the devil and makes people cheerful. Then one forgets all wrath, impurity, sycophancy, and other vices."

Henry Ward Beecher, a colonial minister in New England, wrote: "Hymns are the jewels which the church has worn, the pearls, the diamonds, the precious stones, formed into amulets more potent against sorrow and sadness than the most famous charm of the wizard or the magician."

It is the music that creates the mood in worship and sets the stage for the sermon of the word. Songs of praise pulsate with power and set the human spirit afire. And, when needed, songs of comfort release the tenseness and tightness from the restless heart. Dr. Fredrick Norstad, one of my seminary professors, told of his daughter's courageous battle with cancer. As she was dying, she requested to hear a certain song once more. As she slipped into eternity she rode on the melody and message of the Christmas cradle hymn:

Be near me, Lord Jesus; I ask thee to stay
Close by me for ever, and love me, I pray.

Bless all the dear children in thy tender care,
And fit us for heaven, to live with thee there.

Thankfulness in the heart needs to burst out. Music is the natural way. Let it minister to you and then may you minister to others with all the music you can muster up in your soul. And that deep source of gratitude will flow even in the midst of suffering that may attempt to dry you up. Martin Rinkart, 17th-century preacher, gave us a great hymn during the time of war, famine, and pestilence when he had to bury many loved ones. It goes like this:

Now thank we all our God
With heart and hands and voices,
Who wondrous things hath done,
In whom his world rejoices;
Who, from our mother's arms,
Hath blessed us on our way
With countless gifts of love,
And still is ours today.

Let our singing have less pleading and more praising!

Gratitude rides on the wings of a melody.

18 | Say it with hugs and kisses

And they all wept and embraced Paul and kissed him (Acts 20:37).

Greet one another with the kiss of love (1 Peter 5:14).

Paul was leaving Ephesus where he had established a strong congregation of caring people. The leaders of the church went down to the seaport to bid him goodbye. How were they to thank him for his service amongst them? They prayed together, and tears flowed. Then they embraced and kissed.

A minister went to visit an elderly lady who was confined to her home. Many of her friends had died. Her family lived in another part of the country. Loneliness had moved in and occupied the house and her heart. As the minister sat down and visited, the two of them took a trip together down memory lane. The visit was indeed a pleasant outing. After considerable time, the pastor looked at his watch and told her that he must be on his way. A short devotional was used to cap off the visit. As he rose to leave,

y often come from a lack of
daughter may go off to college.
ivities and pleasures of his new
nk about the love of his parents
call or a letter. A lack of imagi-
sitivity. A few interludes of in-
llow the youth to paint a picture
erhaps respond with some com-
cerned parents.

ned a fine home became dissatisfied
d a better one. He hired an agent
rtisement describing his house and
was ready, the agent showed it to
arefully read it. Surprisingly he re-
think I'll sell this place. I've been
me like that all my life, and I didn't
it." Now that may be a bit absurd!
that frequently, because of lack of
don't see what we have at the end

ts occurred in part of San Francisco
summer season. One merchant had his
windows broken, and part of his store
Things were in total shambles, and he
ut quitting. But then his imagination
, and he came up with an idea. The next
passersby were surprised and amused to
n, crudely painted, in front of the build-

he noticed the furrows that time had etched on her
face. Then he saw the twinkle of gratitude in her
eyes for his visit. He bent over and spontaneously
gave her a kiss on the cheek. She glowed with a shy
little smile and said, "Thank you, thank you. You
see, nobody ever kisses me anymore."

I came from a three-boy family in which kissing
was a sort of lost art. There was a lot of love but little
physical demonstration of it by my brothers and me.
There was much handshaking and many short expressions of "I love you" as we left home after visits.
But it stopped there. Not long ago my mother had
a stroke and was confined to a nursing home in our
hometown in southwestern Minnesota. After each
visit with Mom there was no way that a handshake
could suffice to let her know that I loved her and was
thankful for all she meant to me. Then there were
kisses. And kisses do not cease to be precious when
they cease to be rare.

A few years ago we went to visit a former pastor
associate who was fishing for muskies in northern
Wisconsin. As we arrived at the lake, this big burly-
chested clergyman came bouncing up from where
he was docking his boat and gave me a big bear hug.
A symbol of solidifying friendship, the hug was quite
appropriate. Today we are often embarrassed in
showing affection, afraid it will be misunderstood.
So much devious behavior and so much shallow ro-
mance abound today that we Christians have aban-
doned some of God's beautiful ways of showing
gratitude.

God has never stopped using physical means to show he cares. In Holy Communion he comes through the bread and the wine to touch me. My senses become alive to his pardoning and providing presence. God uses physical vehicles to express his love. That frees me up. There is often a distance between people that is difficult to fill with words. The bridge built by a Christian hug and kiss enables gratitude to travel freely between caring people. William James has said, "Never suffer yourself to have an emotion without giving expression to it."

Thanksgiving travels on tangible expressions.

OPEN FOR BUSINESS!
MORE OPEN THAN USUAL!
Come in and see why some folks just couldn't
wait to get some of our merchandise!

His cheerful acceptance of calamity and quick wit of imagination brought much business. Even some of the looted goods were returned.

Imagination opens up a world of possibilities as it keeps us from pessimism. And as we imagine the power of God, an upward pull occurs in our lives.

The sea of imagination spawns possibilities of praise.

20 | Say it with yourself

Yield yourselves to God as men who have been brought from death to life, and your members to God as instruments of righteousness (Rom. 6:13b).

John Bunyan, author of the famous *Pilgrim's Progress,* did not always have an easy life. Although he was even cast into prison because of the Christian beliefs he held and proclaimed, he also experienced good days, and honors were heaped upon him. One time when lavish praise was pronounced upon him, he said, "I am only God's fiddle, the instrument on which he has elected to play his tunes." And, consequently, his life became an inspiration and comfort to others on their pilgrimage of life.

Yielding yourself to God as an instrument is a beautiful way of saying thanks to God for his goodness. I remember an incident in the first year of my ministry that declared to me how an older brother said thanks to a younger brother for just being a brother. My brother John had purchased a big Oldsmobile which at that time was considered a luxury vehicle. He and his wife were taking a vacation by plane, and he asked me to drive them to the airport. As I dropped them off he said, "By the way, Jim, use my Oldsmobile all you want when we are gone." I was amazed! It was brand-new, and he was telling me to use it and enjoy it.

Well, God certainly does not need cars, but he does want the vehicles of the human vessel to do his business. Paul thus exhorts the church at Rome to "present your bodies as a living sacrifice, holy and acceptable to God, which is your spiritual worship" (Rom. 12:1). No more dead animals on the altar. The new covenant, based on the completed sacrifice of Christ, now asked humanity to offer living, vital service to God. "The members of the body," as Calvin pointed out, "are the instruments by which we execute our purposes." Dedication to God becomes manifest in the availability of your life to fulfill his purposes. An old adage says it: "The only real gift is a portion of yourself."

During the Dark Ages shafts of light did pierce through. Some people in that period were known as "God's merry men." These were the followers of Francis of Assisi. This leader requested his followers to leave behind all gloom and sadness and to participate in new adventures in the spirit of Christ. Long, dull faces would have no part in these ranks. He summoned them to be *joculatores Domini*, which may be translated into English as "the Lord's merry men" or "minstrels of the Lord." Perhaps there could be no better way of expressing thanks to God than spreading a merry heart to disillusioned and disheartened people.

The St. Francis prayer was simple:

> Lord, make me an instrument of thy peace;
> Where there is hatred, let me sow love;
> Where there is injury, pardon;
> Where there is doubt, faith;
> Where there is despair, hope;
> Where there is darkness, light;
> And where there is sadness, joy.
>
> O divine Master,
> Grant that I may not so much seek
> To be consoled, as to console;
> To be understood, as to understand;
> To be loved, as to love.
> For it is in giving that we receive;
> It is in pardoning that we are pardoned;
> It is in dying unto ourselves
> That we are born to eternal life. Amen

Gratitude that lives, gives.

SAY IT IN . . .

Give thanks in all circumstances; *for this is the will of God in Christ Jesus for you.*

1 Thessalonians 5:18

And whatever you do, in word or deed, *do everything* in the name of the Lord Jesus, *giving thanks to God the Father through him.*

Colossians 3:17

In everything *by prayer and supplication with thanksgiving let your requests be made known to God.*

Philippians 4:6

Seasonings are used in foods to add a bit of taste and relish. Without them many dishes would no longer be delicious, but rather they would be drab, dull, and insipid. Consequently, much table talk includes, "Will you please pass the salt?"

The seasoning for all seasons is gratitude. When it is sprinkled into all the situations of life, the environment is enriched and the days are brightened.

21 | Say it in attitude

Not that I complain of want; for
I have learned, in whatever state
I am, to be content (Phil. 4:11).

Emerson once said, "I cannot hear what you are saying for what you are keeps ringing in my ears." Daily attitude sometimes betrays our finest thankful talk. A pulpit full of praise will not undo a week full of murmuring.

The people of Israel had been miraculously delivered by the hand of God through the Red Sea. They sang a great song of salvation, and one would think they would live a long time in the shadow of this providential care. That was not the case, for their water supply ran low, and the water of Marah was bitter. "And the people murmured against Moses" (Exod. 15:24). Soon their food supply dwindled, and again the people murmured. God supplied them both times, first with water and then with manna. But I am sure their attitude sorrowed the heart of God.

Two men will look through the same bars; the one will see mud, the other stars. Two girls may be eating grapes. One will delight in their flavor while the other will be disgusted with their seeds. Two people might be looking at some radiant roses. One will stand in awe of their intricate beauty and refreshing fragrance. The other will complain because the roses have thorns. What makes the difference? It is simply a matter of attitude toward life.

From whence does a bad attitude come? Sometimes it springs from a lack of trust in God. We forget his previous manifestations of power and his present promises of help. Sometimes we forget to think and thus lose our attitude of thanks. We need to count our blessings and name them one by one. Lew Wallace once said, "In thankfulness for present blessings nothing so becomes us as to forget past ills." Sometimes the sin of covetousness creeps into the soul, suffocating any small plants of gratitude. Saul uttered words of discontent when the women praised David more than him. A man complained to Christ, "Teacher, bid my brother divide the inheritance with me." Jesus answered, "Beware of covetousness" (Luke 12:13-15).

A story is told about Abraham Lincoln and his sons. The boys were crying, and a neighbor asked Abe what the problem was. "Just what is the matter with the whole world!" answered Lincoln. "I have three walnuts, and each boy wants two."

As Christians we have a responsibility to concentrate on the construction of a thankful attitude. Erskine Mason said, "Bless God for what you have, and trust God for what you want. If we cannot bring our condition to our mind, we must bring our mind to our condition."

A Swedish proverb says, "Those who wish to sing can always find a song." Two grasshoppers fell into a bowl of cream. One sighed, cried, moaned, and complained and sank to the bottom. The other remained cheerful, kicking his feet, churning the cream until it became butter. He then jumped off the butter to freedom. If we cultivate a contented attitude in our troubles, they just may become stepping-stones rather than tripping-stones.

One thing is needful—a thankful heart.

22 | Say it in victory

But thanks be to God, who gives us the victory through our Lord Jesus Christ (1 Cor. 15:57).

You may think that thanksgiving would automatically flow fast and free when a person stands in the victor's circle. That is not necessarily so! In the aura of achievement humanity is severely tempted by haughtiness. The Lord had to constantly remind the people of Israel not to forget his providence and power when they would bask in the bounty of the promised land. As their enemies tumbled before them and prosperity perched at their doorsteps, the warning of God came: "Beware lest you say in your heart, 'My power and the might of my hand have gotten me this wealth.' You shall remember the Lord your God, for it is he who gives you power to get wealth" (Deut. 8:17-18).

One of the amazing military stories of the Old Testament pits Gideon's troops against the mighty men of the Midianite forces. As the battle drew near, the problem was one of reducing the number of the

Israelite army rather than recruiting more foot soldiers. The reason given for this maneuver was, "lest
Israel vaunt themselves against me, saying 'My own
hand has delivered me' " (Judg. 7:2). God knew that
if Israel thought deliverance came only by her own
strength, the experience might carry her further
from God instead of bringing her nearer. Thus the
army had to be small so they knew, beyond doubt,
that defeat would be inevitable without divine aid.

Gideon had the job of reducing the ranks which
numbered 32,000. He asked if there were soldiers who
faced the battle with fear and trembling. Twenty-
two thousand stepped forward, and they were sent
home. Still too many. The number was drastically cut
back when he had the remaining soldiers drink from
a running brook. Everyone who knelt down, probably laying aside his weapons, was dismissed. Those
who cupped water in their hands and lapped, like a
dog alert to danger, remained. The remnant of soldiers going to battle against the Midianites totaled 300.
The contest seemed absurd since the enemy looked
like "locusts for multitude." However, Gideon and
his mighty minority maneuvered a military victory
and routed the Midianites, and they knew it was a
gift from God!

An old fable tells about a briar bush that was dug
up from an old roadside and transplanted in a beautiful botanical garden. There the gardener grafted a
radiant rose branch into the briar bush. Not long afterward a beautiful rose bud appeared on the twisted,
scraggy bush. The bush began to brag to the rest of

the garden about his beauty. The gardener overheard his boisterous talk. He reminded the bush that his beauty did not come from his own doing, but rather was the result of what the gardener put into him.

The grateful person sees that achievements and victories are not accomplished in an isolation ward. We all owe our lives, our food, our jobs, our joys, our pleasures, our education, and our opportunities to others and to God. Many of the blessings come through distant and different races and cultures. Victories in the life of any individual come only as the result of team assistance. And a better world will be built when we all say with the Apostle Paul, "I am under obligation both to Greeks and to barbarians, both to the wise and to the foolish" (Rom. 1:14).

Gratitude lives in indebtedness.

23 | Say it in prayer

Have no anxiety about anything, but in everything by prayer and supplication with thanksgiving let your requests be known to God (Phil. 4:6).

A fine college choir was going to perform at our church. Prior to the concert they were downstairs in the church warming up their voices. They had a trial run on some of their selections and then paused for a moment of prayer before they came into the sanctuary for the concert. They evidently felt a need to be properly prepared before they ministered to the congregation in song.

Before the umpires shout, "Play ball!" there is always a warm-up session on the field of play. The players limber up their bodies and sharpen their batting eyes. The pitcher loosens up his arm before he begins to throw his lightning-fast pitches. If a game is to be well played, there must be adequate preparation.

Life can be compared to a stage on which the great

drama is enacted. It can also be likened to a field of play on which we are the participants. If so, then the warm-up sessions are just as necessary for us all as for the musicians and the baseball players. Prayer becomes that period of getting prepared. Jesus spent time communicating with the Father before all the major events of his ministry.

Dr. Alexis Carrell, a great physician and Nobel Prize winner, said, "Prayer is the most powerful form of energy that man can generate. The influence of prayer on the mind and body is as demonstrable as secreting glands. Its results can be measured in terms of increased buoyancy, greater intellectual vigor, moral stamina, and a deeper understanding of human relationships." Jenny Lind, the late great opera star, always would spend a few moments of quietness before every performance. This Swedish nightingale, in the privacy of her dressing room, would strike one clear note and hold it as long as she could. Then she would pray, "Master, let me ring true tonight. Let me ring true, as thou art true."

Prayer will thus condition the mind and body and prepare it for the task ahead. There is a slogan that is used on many plaques: Prayer changes things. There is truth to that. But it is also true that prayer perhaps more frequently changes people, and people change things.

It is at this point that Paul urges us to have "prayer with thanksgiving." Thankfulness becomes the tuning fork which we use to set the tone for daily life. Prayer is not a bombarding of heaven with one petition after another. Surely God wants us to ask for what we need, but the depth of prayer is more profound. Prayer for a grateful heart can actually change the chemistry of your cranium so you see causes for thankful living in all situations.

Maybe an example will help. Dandelions are weeds which most people try to eradicate from their lawns. Their roots go deep, and they have an uncanny ability to invade and conquer in the battle with the grasses. In the spring of the year their yellow flowers smile at the faces of young children romping in the out-of-doors. They become irresistible, and your child picks them with glee, bringing you a bouquet of these "weeds." Do you scold your child and then throw the weeds in the trash? Of course not! You smile and say thank you for the lovely flowers. You take down a vase and put the dandelions in it and place it on the kitchen table. Why? Simply because you see in the dandelions the delight of your child and the love your child has for you. That love conditions your view of the weeds.

Prayers, which tune up your thankful heart, enable you to face life and all of its weeds with a spirit of gratitude.

Your mental motor needs frequent tune-ups of thanksgiving.

24 | Say it in all seasons

I have learned, in whatever state I am, to be content (Phil. 4:11).

Giving thanks in all circumstances, as Paul did, is a difficult assignment. However, when it is done, the atmosphere in the classroom of life changes from one of pessimism to optimism. Complaints become less frequent, and cheers are on the increase.

We have become conditioned into thinking that there are special times that are designated for gratitude. Christmas seems to top the list, nosing out Thanksgiving Day by a narrow margin. We show our thankfulness for family and friends with a profuse display of presents and pronouncements of goodwill. We crawl out of the cave of selfishness and blink our eyes at a day of gratitude and cheer. We say thanks to those whom we might otherwise ignore or at best tolerate. Of course, there are other appropriate times in which to make our thank-you declarations. When there are birthdays, holidays, and other celebrations, gratitude is quite fitting and natural.

But it is in those extra times, those unexpected moments, when you don't have to do it but you want to do it, that gratitude makes life richer for God and his people. I like strawberries, most available in May and June in Minnesota where I live. Homegrown, they can become routine in their season. But serve up a dish in January! That is the height of luxury. Corn on the cob in July and August is common enough. But good corn on the cob in midwinter is something extra.

When Oliver Cromwell was dying and his bed was surrounded by mournful faces, he looked up and said, "Will no one here thank God?" Such a statement was not expected. Yet how refreshing it was during a melancholy mood. In times of health, prosperity, and good fortune it is easy to put in a word of thanks. In times of pain, poor health, and pressure the word of thanks comes with more difficulty. But it also packs a greater punch and a pleasant surprise.

It must please God to see his children love him by showing thanks in season and out of season. Their gratitude is measured neither by the calendar nor the thermometer. Like a magnet pulling out iron pieces in the sand, their grateful hearts pull out reason for thanksgiving in all circumstances. You become doubly blessed when you render thanks not only in the routine of the expected but also in the realm of the unexpected.

Gratitude is a seasoning for all seasons.

25 | Say it in youth

Then children were brought to him that he might lay his hands on them and pray. The disciples rebuked the people; but Jesus said, "Let the children come to me, and do not hinder them; for to such belongs the kingdom of heaven" (Matt. 19:13-14).

Rejoice, O young man, in your youth, and let your heart cheer you in the days of your youth (Eccles. 11:9).

Maurice Chevalier, French actor and singer, made famous the song, "Thank Heaven for Little Girls." But today there do not seem to be many little girls, or for that matter, little boys, around anymore. A man recently was asked, "How old is your daughter?" He replied, "Twelve, going on twenty!" There seems to be a real confusion here as we reach for maturity even before the ripening process should start taking place. A twelve year old went shopping and on her list was the following: "Water pistol, brassiere, and permanent."

Remember the Red Queen? She is the one who took Alice by the hand and dragged her at top speed through the Looking-Glass land. She was always crying, "Faster! Faster! Don't try to talk. Faster!" She was a fine and funny imaginary character in fairy-tale land. The problem is that we have adapted her philosophy in real life so that we push children into adult shoes just as fast as they can stumble into them. And they don't fit!

The thought of childhood used to conjure up pleasant memories of long, lazy days with a bit of mischief sandwiched between them. Today things get so organized with music lessons, little league sports, and a host of other scheduled activities that unadorned childhood is missing. Children are labeled as preschool, preteen, and preadult. We ask them why they don't act their age. The truth is that they probably are doing just that, but we usually want them to be at a more advanced stage.

Maybe Raggedy Ann dolls of olden days will make a comeback. They were made of soft stuff. Children could hug them, care for them, and use them for pillows. A great deal of imaginative pretending occurred with those dolls. Then came the era of Barbie and her descendants. No longer were the dolls soft and cuddly. They became miniatures of real movie stars. They had faces, figures, and hair that the adults would envy. Although the Barbie doll craze was a bonanza to the business world, it certainly didn't do much for the children's world.

I advocate letting children be children and letting them be thankful for days of freewheeling time when they can play in their sandboxes and make their sand castles. Children should be able to waste a summer afternoon without feeling guilty or ride their bikes nowhere just for the fun of it. They shouldn't have to make up their minds right away. And as adults we should thank God for those years when children can pause along the way and savor the present without always being urged to look to some future time. Let's give them back a Raggedy Ann doll!

A child at play is a picture of gratitude to the creator.

26 | Say it in old age

I have been young, and now am old; yet I have not seen the righteous forsaken or his children begging bread. He is ever giving liberally and lending, and his children become a blessing (Ps. 37:25-26).

In the springtime of life when the buds are bursting and flowers are filled with fragrance, it is relatively easy to give thanks. When the cold winds of winter begin to blow across the landscape of life and everything begins to stiffen up, it is more of a struggle to break out into songs of thanksgiving. But it is exactly then that the grace of God enables gratitude to keep growing. The old have much to give as the mellow harvest of wisdom is gathered in the storehouse of the mind and soul. The psalmist pictures the elderly as contributing much, "giving liberally and lending."

In a Peanuts comic strip, Lucy asks Charlie Brown, "Do you think life has its peaks and valleys?" The answer is affirmative. Lucy replies, "Then, that means that there must be one day above all others in each life that is the happiest, right?" Charlie responds, "I guess that is true." Then Lucy sadly says, "What if you've already had it?"

In an age which idolizes youth there is a temptation to think that the good times belong to youth, and dregs are deposited in old age. God wants us to keep growing as long as we live. I love the lesson from the life of Grandma Moses who began her incredible career of painting at age 78. A reporter said, "She kept on learning and improving, and hit her stride around 85."

When my father was sick with Parkinson's disease, he received a letter from a 91-year-old friend who expressed thankfulness in old age. Here are some of his statements:

This afternoon I shall venture out and take a little visit with you. I am thinking so much of you and praying for you in the morning and evening at devotional time, thinking of your trouble and fight for life. I pray that God will stand by you when the burdens begin to press. I know he will for there are no shortcomings with the Father. His hand is there at the right time.

I am also among the shut-ins and can't get around any more. I am set on the shelf, pushed back as far as I will go. But I am not alone. My Heavenly Father, who has stood by me these ninety-one years, stands by me now. He is wonderful. When I see his smiling face, my heart begins to bubble. I realize my days are almost up. I look at the trees along the street that stand there so naked, hardly a leaf left. I said to myself that I am like them. Not many leaves left. Soon the last one will fall, and I will be laid away.

But here I am today, rejoicing in the Lord. If I had a thousand lives yet to live I would hold on to my Saviour's hand all the more. Nothing is better. So Johs, I will meet you in the morning when the sun shall never set. Till then, keep looking up.

Grow old along with me!
The best is yet to be,
The last of life, for which the first was made:
Our times are in his hand
Who saith "A whole I planned,
Youth shows but half; trust God:
    see all, nor be afraid!"

                              Robert Browning

Gratitude never rots, it only ripens with age.

27 | Say it in good fortune

Every good endowment and every perfect gift is from above, coming down from the Father of lights (James 1:17).

It is easy for man to develop such an inflated sense of his own importance and ingenuity that he takes everything good that happens to him as if it were his due. He believes he deserves the best. The attitude of taking credit for good things creeps over his cranium and suffocates the seed of gratitude.

A scientist has figured out that a farmer's effort is only about five percent of the total factors which produce wheat. Yet how many bow before a meal and give thanks to the ninety-five percent contribution of the Creator?

The Israelites were severely tempted by self-sufficiency as they moved into the good land of promise under the leadership of Moses and then Joshua. A warning from God was issued to them: "Take heed lest you forget the Lord your God . . . when you have eaten and are full, and have built goodly houses and lived in them, and when your herds and flocks multiply, and your silver and gold is multiplied, and all that you have is multiplied. . . . Beware lest you say in your heart, 'My power and the might of my hand have gotten me this wealth.' " (Deut. 8:11-13, 17).

The ground rule of gratitude is that we never forget that "in him we live and move and have our being" (Acts 17:28). Gratitude is an attitude of dependency. A scoutmaster told his boys that when they were in the woods they should always remember that they were guests of the animals, plants, and trees.

I have often wondered why only one of the ten lepers that were cleansed by Jesus came back and gave thanks. Maybe some of them believed more in luck, coincidence, and chance than they did in the Good Physician. Could it be that some of them were so blinded that they would blurt out: "Well, I'm not sure it was Jesus who healed me. I know I talked to him and he touched me and shortly afterwards my body began to heal. But that may have been coincidence. You know you can't keep a good man down forever. I always did believe that sooner or later I could lick this thing if I didn't give up." In such an attitude the adoration of God is abolished.

People show amazing potential in the world of business, discovery, arts, and athletics. But in all these things they are merely developing the resources that God has given to them. All good fortune must go back to the founding Father.

Gratitude is a declaration of dependence.

28 | Say it in marriage

Therefore a man leaves his father and his mother and cleaves to his wife, and they become one flesh (Gen. 2:24).

Husbands, love your wives, as Christ loved the church and gave himself up for her (Eph. 5:25).

We were created in such a way that a male and a female could form a balanced whole in a relationship called marriage. Like my two eyes or my two arms or my two legs work together in unity, so, too, the two sexes are not to be competitors but companions. Each can fortify and fulfill the other. Each one complements and supplements the other. At least that is the way God intended it to be. But marriage, like other mechanisms, can be marred by malfunctioning. It requires constant maintenance to keep it performing. Otherwise it will have a breakdown, or we might, as Thoreau stated, "Live quiet lives of desperation."

At most marriage ceremonies there is an abundance of flowers. They appear in bouquets, bundles, and boutonnieres. Having been cut from their source of life, they last as long as some marriages which start to die at the altar. Because they are rooted and receive the rain which naturally refreshes them, flowers in the garden live and continue to grow and blossom. If there is a rainless period, the gardener takes out a hose and gives them a drink. Marriages are something like the ever-present flowers. They will receive no automatic rains from the sky to keep them alive, but must be watered regularly by the two who enter into the holy estate.

How do you water a marriage? A mate compliments rather than criticizes. He communicates at the gut level rather than circumcising all issues. She doesn't worry about who is the better half. A good marriage is the union of two good forgivers. And all kinds of physical manifestations water a marriage. You don't have to be sexual gymnasts after 20 years of marriage in order to have contentment. However, you can still learn new tricks of fulfilling each other, and the old ones will also continue to work. It has been said that most marital graves are not made by one big excavation but by a series of little digs. I believe it to be true. Likewise, good marriages don't happen overnight. Good marriages are not made in heaven. They come, as much merchandise does today, in kits. You have to put it together yourself. In order to have a good mate you must be one yourself.

An old Swedish couple had been married for 40

years. They had never been happy with each other although they were sticking it out together. They argued, quarreled, and found fault with each other. Finally Inga said to Sven, "Sven, this thing is not working. We been married for 40 years now. We tried everything. We always fighting. Why don't we pray to the good Lord to take one of us home, and then I can go and live with my sister."

They were reaping what they sowed—selfishness. My father once told me that God had given him a beautiful gift in my mother. That was the secret! You say thanks for gifts. When you keep saying it to each other in imaginative ways all the days of your marriage, the marriage will always stay fresh and fragrant.

Gratitude each day keeps divorce away.

29 | Say it in all places

> *Sing to the Lord a new song, his praise from the end of the earth!
> ... Let the inhabitants of Sela sing for joy, let them shout from the top of the mountains. Let them give glory to the Lord, and declare his praise in the coastlands* (Isa. 42:10-12).

Praise to God is neither just a private affair nor is it to be limited to a particular place. The psalmist informs us that praise should stretch from the countryside to the coastlands and into the cities. We have often boxed it up in a worship service at church where it seems proper and less conspicuous to the world. But the lilting language of praise is too big to be confined by the limits of liturgy. It is also to be performed on the streets.

Kipling has a poem entitled, "Mulholland's Contract." Mulholland was a cattleman on a ship, and his place was in the hold where the cattle were carried across the sea. One day a devastating storm was devouring the ship with mighty waves. When the cattle broke loose from their pens, panic prevailed. In the midst of the stampeding cattle and flailing hoofs, it seemed certain that Mulholland would be killed. He then prayed to God, making a contract that if God would get him to the port alive he would spend the rest of his life praising his name. Miraculously he was preserved. When on shore, Mulholland waited for his orders from God, thinking that he would be preaching Christ in some handsome cathedral. But the answer came back to him:

> I never puts on my ministers
> no more than they can bear.
> So back you go to the cattleboats
> and preach My Gospel there.

It was not for Mulholland to find an easier sphere to spread the praise of God; he was to do it in the place where he was. When Jesus had restored to sanity the madman who had been living amongst the tombs of the cemetery, the man requested that he be allowed to go with Jesus and remain with him. Jesus gave him a quick answer, "Go home to your friends, and tell them how much the Lord has done for you, and how he has had mercy on you" (Mark 5:19).

In unexpected places and at unexpected times praise to God is most potent. It might be easiest to say a prayer of thanks for a meal in the privacy of your home. But why not let your light of gratitude shine in the public place of a restaurant? It is easiest to present a platitude of praise in a *Bible* class setting. But why not show your Christian colors while sitting in the chair of business?

A Welsh miner was converted during a revival. His fellow workers thought they would test the reality of it by checking his usual vehement reactions. They stole his dinner pail before the noon lunch break. They expected him to break out in an angry oath when he discovered it missing. They were totally surprised when he just smiled and said, "Praise the Lord! I've still got my appetite. They can't take that!" You can't beat the working world for an appropriate place for praise.

The place for praise is your present address.

30 | Say it in suffering

> *More than that, we rejoice in our*
> *sufferings, knowing that suffering*
> *produces endurance, and endur-*
> *ance produces character, and char-*
> *acter produces hope, and hope does*
> *not disappoint us, because God's*
> *love has been poured into our*
> *hearts through the Holy Spirit*
> *which has been given to us* (Rom.
> 5:3-5).

Have you ever gone in search of
suffering so that you might have cause for rejoicing?
Of course not! Such a suggestion is absurd. You don't
seek out either a blot on your reputation or a bleeding
ulcer. You don't try to secure a tragic accident or a
trauma of the mind. But storms of suffering do come
on the sea of life. Some swing into our serene setting
by our own stupidity; then the crises come from our
carelessness. Some suffering arrives at our residence
because of the irresponsibility of others. But much
suffering cannot be labeled with a causative factor. It

just happens in a broken world that has been severed by sin. Once when Jesus told his disciples to cross the Sea of Galilee, they were engulfed by wild winds and waves. They were merely in the process of obeying a command of Christ. Yet, even at such a time, they were not immune from the trial of trouble.

We, therefore, must not spend hours of time either accusing ourselves or excusing ourselves when suffering stops at our doorsteps. We must move quickly from the cause of the crisis to the challenge of the crisis. In the realm the Christian life, the Apostle Paul testifies that suffering can produce a chain of events as it moves from endurance to character and ends up with hope. But that doesn't automatically happen as you sit with folded hands and a pious expression on your face. Suffering in itself does not necessarily strengthen character. It may break and embitter a person's spirit. Its results depend entirely on the way in which suffering is accepted. You may cower in a cave of self-pity in the face of crisis. Or you may confront the crisis from the standpoint of not what it is going to do to you but rather what you are going to do with it. Lord Reith once said, "I do not like crises, but I do like the opportunities they provide."

We must face suffering like Jacob of old when wrestling with the angel. Jacob was in pain—his thigh was out of joint. However, he held on to his opponent saying, "I will not let you go, unless you bless me" (Gen. 32:26). The state of mind with which we step into the arena of suffering becomes all-important. The challenge lies in not running away,

in believing the fact of it, and in not blaming someone else for what has happened. It is in facing the
crisis that we take the wound and wrestle a victory
from it. Although at the time our vision might be
blurred, God can provide us with new opportunities
for life and growth in these experiences.

A tiny grain of sand, an alien thing, intrudes into
the privacy of an oyster. The oyster accepts the pain,
and with layers of a milky-like, plastic substance, it
covers the grain of sand until it is transformed into
a pearl. A low intensity fire in a forest can clean up
the clutter on the forest floor without destroying the
huge trees. The forest undergrowth will then be
cleared, the hard-shelled seed coats of fire-dependent
species will be broken, and new seedbeds prepared. As
it happens in nature, so can it happen in me. The
psalmist put it this way, "Before I was afflicted I went
astray; but now I keep thy word" (Ps. 119:67).

A spirit of gratitude toward life always keeps you
looking for something good in the midst of the bad.
You don't have to thank God for the crisis but by
thanking him in it you will accept it as a challenge
rather than a curse.

*Thanksgiving can transform a tragedy into a
triumph.*

SAY IT TO . . .

We are bound to give thanks to God always for you, brethren, as is fitting, because your faith is growing abundantly, and the love of every one of you for one another is increasing.

2 THESSALONIANS 1:3

Dostoyevsky tells about a woman evangelist who, with great zeal, traveled through Russia telling about the love of God. Yet she could not stand being in a room for very long with any other person. One man slurped his soup and that irritated her. One woman cackled when she laughed and that bothered her. Another man would snore in his sleep and that disturbed her peace of mind. Dostoyevsky said, "Although she loved God in general, she couldn't stand human beings in particular."

That is quite a predicament! It is also easy to be thankful in general; it's more difficult to be specific. But that is what we need to do. Saying thank you person to person is what is pleasing to God.

31 | Say it to God the Father

*He shall cry to me, "Thou art my
Father, my God, and the Rock of
my salvation"* (Ps. 89:26).

*Yet, O Lord, thou art our Father;
we are the clay, and thou art our
potter; we are all the work of thy
hand* (Isa. 64:8).

It was a gray, overcast day. Mist
was falling, making for a melancholy mood as I drove
on impulse to the tree-covered cemetery outside of
Windom, Minnesota. It had been a favorite play-
ground of mine when I was a small boy. I used to ob-
serve birds, climb trees, dodge among the tombstones,
and drown out gophers that made the cemetery their
home. But on this day, many years later, I had not
come to play. I stopped the car on a little knoll,
stepped outside, and gazed at a stone that had en-
graved on it: A. Johs Bjorge 1895-1966. I stood
pensively for a few moments, looked up toward the
heavens, and said, "Thanks." Then I silently saluted

and slipped away from the still stone resting under a stately pine tree.

The man who was buried there was much more stately to me than the trees that stood there on sentinel duty watching over those plotted acres. I had walked through many woods and fields in the company of one who was an oak of a man. I saw in him good timber—strong and straight and true. He was deep rooted in his faith in the Lord. He was fruitful in his acts of concern that reached into the lives of others. This man taught me how to pray. He showed me how to bait a fishhook, shoot a gun, and simply to enjoy nature. He raced down the street with me, punched me in the nose while boxing, spanked me, and held me in his lap. He gave me big bear hugs. He loved his family and made our house a home always worth coming back to.

Yes, he was an oak of a man. He was my father. That stone in the cemetery tells me where we put his body. But he isn't there. Those dates on the tombstone cannot box in his influence. Neither do they measure his growth. "He is like a tree planted by streams of water, that yields its fruit in its season, and its leaf does not wither" (Ps. 1:3). I know he still loves me wherever he is in that vast empire of God's eternal kingdom.

I am fortunate, indeed, to have had an earthly father who became a window through whom I could readily see and understand my heavenly Father. Jesus taught us to pray, "Our Father who art in heaven. . . ." The words come easily to me, for the images of a caring earthly father became the mental building blocks that constructed an understanding of God, the Father Almighty.

Charles Spurgeon, a noted English clergyman, noticed that the weather vane on the roof of a farm building bore the phrase "God is love." He was troubled by this. "Do you think God's love is as changeable as that weather vane?" he asked the farmer. "You miss the point, sir," replied the farmer. "It's on the weather vane because no matter which way the wind is blowing, God is still love." My heavenly Father is, "The Father of lights with whom there is no variation or shadow due to change" (James 1:17).

His arms constantly hold me, and his lap is always big enough for all his children. Maybe the best way I can say thanks to him is merely to be as a child who climbs into his lap and clings to his tender care.

Thanksgiving is a child in father's lap.

32 | Say it to Jesus Christ

Thanks be to God through Jesus Christ our Lord (Rom. 7:25a).

Class reunions are exercises in nostalgia. They are set up to create warm feelings around the heart and screen out unpleasant memories. No lies are told, but everybody seems to remember big! Remembering is fun as we recall old professors and ancient pranks. We can never reclaim that time in history, but going home can be good, even as we are reminded that we now have new homes, new lives, and new duties to perform.

I recently attended my 30th high school class reunion. I spent considerable time talking to a psychiatrist who was, as a young lad, my best friend. In the conversation he brought up an incident which happened when we were sitting next to each other in choir. Neither one of us was blessed with a good singing voice, so our attention was not always very intent. One day I made a bit of noise and began to sing off-key (not a very difficult thing for me to do). The choir director reacted very quickly. The problem was that she thought the culprit was my friend. He was immediately expelled from choir for a few days' duration. Due to my lack of heroics and also my glee at getting one-up on my friend who loved practical jokes, I did not volunteer that I was the guilty one. Surprisingly, my friend accepted the penalty for me, and the director never was aware that a substitute took the blame.

As my wife and I drove home that night, the thought occurred to me that someone else also stepped into my life and took the blame for all my sin and shortcoming. He didn't have to do it, but he loved me and did not want to see the penalty of eternal death come down on me. His name is Jesus! He said, "I am the good shepherd; I know my own and my own know me, as the Father knows me and I know the Father; and I lay down my life for the sheep" (John 10:14-15).

As I think back on those younger days of my life I also recall a neighborhood fight in which I was involved. It was a rough-and-tumble affair, and I was coming out second best. In the closing minutes of this childhood struggle my opponent was beginning to choke me. At that moment my big brother, who had been observing this battle of boys, stepped forward and rescued me. What if my brother had not been there? But he was! He has always seemed to be there in the crucible of every crisis that I have encountered in my young and adult life. Jesus has been that kind of brother too. When I falter and when I fear, he is there to comfort, strengthen, and cheer. He promised all his children, "Lo, I am with you always" (Matt. 28:20).

I had a friend who was willing to take my blame. I have a brother who sticks by in time of need. Well, Jesus Christ is both to me and yet more. As I thank my earthly friends and brothers, I do not forget to look up and simply say, "Thank you, too, Jesus!"

Surely he has borne our griefs
    and carried our sorrows; . . .
But he was wounded for our transgressions,
    he was bruised for our iniquities;
upon him was the chastisement
that made us whole,
    and with his stripes we are healed. . . .
He was oppressed, and he was afflicted,
    yet he opened not his mouth;
like a lamb that is led to the slaughter,
    and like a sheep that before
    its shearers is dumb,
so he opened not his mouth.

Isaiah 53:4-5, 7

Remember to thank your Redeemer.

33 | Say it to the Holy Spirit

But you shall receive power when the Holy Spirit has come upon you; and you shall be my witnesses in Jerusalem and in all Judea and Samaria and to the end of the earth (Acts 1:8).

A child might come home from school and greet his mother with the question, "Have you been doing anything today, Mom?" Because of the child's lack of observation and imagination he does not envision the daily toil of a mother in the home. The washing of dishes and clothes. The ironing, the picking up of messy rooms. The grocery shopping and making of meals. These and countless other tasks are overlooked by the child who seems to think that Mom was sitting on her duff all day.

Perhaps we all are like children when we come into the presence of God. "Hey, Lord, what have you been doing lately?" We seem to forget that he is in charge of this universe and a million or more others. He keeps track of a world of children and not just one household. When we pause to consider it all, we wonder how God has not run himself ragged.

But let us take it down to the personal level. Jesus told us that the Father was sending the Holy Spirit. He is doing many things. Luther, in his catechism, says that the Holy Spirit "has called me through the Gospel, enlightened me with his gifts, and sanctified and kept me in true faith. In the same way he calls, gathers, enlightens, and sanctifies the whole Christian church on earth, and keeps it united with Jesus Christ in the one true faith."

Jesus said, "And when he comes, he will convince the world concerning sin and righteousness and judgment" (John 16:8). As a child of God have you ever wondered why when you do bad things you feel bad? Is it merely the voice or echo of parents and principles which are pronouncing their condemnation? I believe it is more than that! The Holy Spirit is symbolized by a cleansing fire. God the Holy Spirit does not want us to go around with dirty hands and faces. He wants us to clean up our acts. Consequently, when we sin, we feel the tug of God on our shirttails. He does not overlook our transgressions any more than loving parents who want to keep us on the straight and narrow for our own good. Thanks, Holy Spirit, for keeping me in line!

Jesus says the Spirit will also convince us of righteousness. As we read the newspapers, we often have a tendency to think that truth has fallen, and falsehood occupies the throne. Evil seems to prosper, and good seems to be in a recession. In spite of all appearances to the contrary, the Holy Spirit assures us that the wrong shall fail and the right prevail. Jesus will be the last word. Righteousness also means right living. At this point I wonder why it is that I feel good when I have done an act of love in Jesus' name? I believe it is the Holy Spirit who is not so shy that he will not give a person a pat on the back. Thanks, Holy Spirit, for your stamp of approval on right living!

Thirdly, Jesus said the Spirit will convince the world of judgment. It is not enough to say that we ought to be responsible. We are responsible. Daniel Webster once said, "The greatest thought I have had is the realization of my personal responsibility to God." Thanks, Holy Spirit, for the dignity that responsibility places upon me.

So if you are wondering what God is doing, just pause and take a good look into your life. Then thank the Spirit that he is still working with you.

Equal adoration be, Eternal Paraclete, to thee.

34 | Say it to parents

I thank God whom I serve with a clear conscience, as did my fathers, when I remember you constantly in my prayers. . . . I am reminded of your sincere faith, a faith that dwelt first in your grandmother Lois and in your mother Eunice and now, I am sure, dwells in you (2 Tim. 1:3-5).

Shakespeare once said, "Sharper than a serpent's tooth is a thankless child." However, nothing is sweeter and softer than a child's gratitude. It was the final track meet of the season for our senior-class daughter, and the stadium in which it was held was quite a few miles from home. My wife and I drove down to see her run the two-mile event, a long and grueling race. The rain began to cascade down from the canopy of heaven as she commenced her race. My blue dress suit soaked up the rain and sagged on my frame. But I stood there, proud of my daughter. Following the race she rode home with us in the car rather than on the school bus. As we began the trip back she said, "Thanks for coming." I reached my arm around to the back seat and she put her hand in mine. It was a brief moment that was like being on the top of a mountain.

A short time ago I had the privilege of sitting with a family whose mother at the age of 48 was dying of cancer. She was a noble woman who lived her faith and never lowered the flag. They all spoke openly about death. The father and the three children, all college age, expressed their love for each other that evening. Tears of thanksgiving washed all our eyes as we talked together. A while later she died.

At the funeral, the young daughter gave me a letter to read that she and her brothers had written. Here is what it said:

> When we think of Mom we have nice thoughts, happy thoughts. We will miss her and will feel her loss greatly. We admire her strong faith. We know that she is in heaven where she hoped she would be some day. We will miss her strength, optimism and sense of humor.
>
> We are sorry that we won't be able to say "thanks" to Mom anymore. Thanks for raising us in a Christian home. Thanks for having high expectations and a loving understanding of our shortcomings. Thanks for being there to listen, to give advice and be a friend.
>
> We will never be able to repay the love that Mom

gave us. That kind of love isn't repaid. We could only hope to pass it on.

Now is the proper time to say thanks to parents . . . and then pass it on. Jesus said, "As the Father loves me so I love you." God wants the chain of gratitude to continue on from one generation to another.

Gratitude makes parenting a privilege.

35 | Say it to children

If you then, who are evil, know how to give good gifts to your children, how much more will your Father who is in heaven give good things to those who ask him! (Matt. 7:11).

Two of our basic needs are a sense of belonging and self-esteem. Children have voracious appetites for both. They want the security which a loving home can supply. In the midst of their adventures they want a place to roost, a place of belonging. Too many children have picked up the vibes that they were biological "accidents." In the midst of the terrible teens they may hear their parents discussing the idea that they, the parents, should have exercised more careful family planning. Too often, during these formative years, the cup of dignity has been drained by criticism in the lives of youth. They are left dry, and they believe the landscape of their lives will produce little or nothing. A few well-placed comments of gratitude for them will go far in filling up the reservoir of esteem. Benjamin West once said, "It was a mother's kiss that made me a painter."

A few years ago when my brother John and I were working on a manuscript together he wrote an open letter to his three children. I will share it with you:

Good morning! Your father and mother love you very much just because you are you! Maggie and I often thank God for giving us the three of you. You have brought much joy and contentment into our lives.

John, you know that we adopted you. You are "ours." You are a chip off the old block, and you didn't grow under Maggie's heart but in it. Your father has the same wonderful, beautiful vibes toward you as he does toward Lisa and Marit. If someday you have a "need" to find your biological mother and/or father we will not stand in the way, but we want you to know that we love you in the same way we love Lisa and Marit. You are our son. Lisa and Marit are our daughters.

John, Lisa and Marit, your father and mother rejoice with you in your accomplishments and sorrow with you in your failures. Always remember your places in our hearts are secure, being independent of how well you perform. We are following with interest your school work, your extra curricular activities in music and sports, and your growing relationships with people. We wish you well in all your endeavors.

You are not little children any longer. It will not be long before you will be making decisions on your own. We pray we have been helpful in equipping you for good choices. Whether you go to college or not, what college you go to if you go, the type of employment you seek, marrying or staying single, remaining a Christian—these are all decisions we cannot make for you. We do not want to force or coerce you in any manner. We do, however, pray that Jesus Christ will always be the center of your lives and that together we will remain a part of the family of God.

We hope you realize that we love you whether you are good or bad, whether you bring us honor or shame. We want you to be happy, joyous, winsome, wholesome persons with a song on your lips because of knowing who you are, why you are here and where you are going. Forgive us our failures. Thank you for being our son and daughters. Always remember we love you.

A commendation to a child is gratitude communicated.

36 | Say it to the body

For thou didst form my inward parts, thou didst knit me together in my mother's womb. I praise thee, for thou art fearful and wonderful. Wonderful are thy works! Thou knowest me right well; my frame was not hidden from thee, when I was being made in secret, intricately wrought in the depths of the earth (Ps. 139:13-15).

"Mirror, mirror on the wall, who is fairest of them all?" We remember that line in a fairy-tale story from our youth. Being obsessed with one's beauty becomes idolatry. However, being thankful for one's body is a Christian virtue. Feel your pulse. Your heart is pumping blood that surges through a network of veins and arteries. If you live until 75, figuring at a conservative 60 strokes per minute, it would consist of around two and a half billion beats. That is amazing! To top it off, this pump never goes on strike for higher wages, forcing a layoff of legs, liver, or lungs. It follows the instructions of the nervous system without any instruction. Talk about a "faithful heart," folks, you've got it! Have you ever thanked your heart by saying, "Bless my little heart"?

Think of your ears that open up for you a world of thousands of vibrations. You can hear about 11 octaves. Your eyes, even though they might be behind glasses, give you a world of shapes and forms, colors and intricate designs. Your touch can be sensitive enough to read braille or feel the warmth of a hug. When Martin Luther thought of the first article of faith, he thanked God for his body, limbs, and senses, reason and all faculties of the mind.

But how do you give thanks to your body? You must recognize it as a marvelous mechanism made by God. As any other mechanism it needs a good maintenance schedule. To keep it in good condition you must take it out for a walk very frequently. Just as you need to get your car out on the open road at higher rates of speed to get the carbon out, you also need to step up the pace of exercise for your body to "get the lead out," as we used to say to lazy folk. Then you must not make your body a disposal unit for junk foods. You don't use leaded gasoline in cars that call for unleaded. Why do we tank up our systems with that which is toxic to our well-being? You say thanks to your body by keeping it in the best possible condition—clean, well nourished, well exercised, and well groomed.

I have a small chair at home that dates back to the

Napoleonic Wars. It was the only piece of furniture my Dad brought over from Norway. It is a family heirloom. I cherish it. That simply means I care about it and take care of it. In so doing, I show gratitude to the ancestors who passed it down through the years. Do you realize that when you cherish and take care of your body, you are saying thanks to God? Well, you are, because he gave it to you. "Do you not know that your body is a temple of the Holy Spirit within you, which you have from God? You are not your own; you were bought with a price. So glorify God in your body" (1 Cor. 6:19-20).

May the building of the body be a house of gratitude.

37 | Say it to those who serve

We give thanks to God always for you all, constantly mentioning you in our prayers, remembering before our God and Father your work of faith and labor of love and steadfastness of hope in our Lord Jesus Christ (1 Thess. 1:2-3).

Paul was constantly expressing gratitude for fellow laborers in kingdom work. He was bound together with them in a ministry of love. He said, "None of us lives to himself, and none of us dies to himself" (Rom. 14:7). Each is responsible for all, and all are responsible for each one.

In his play *An Inspector Calls*, J. B. Priestly portrays how we can miss the interrelatedness of life. A police inspector calls on a middle-class family following a suicide in the neighborhood. A girl, Eva Smith, has taken her life, and the inspector desires to discover events that led to this tragedy. The father, who owns a small factory, does not recall the name,

117

but, under questioning, realizes that he had fired this girl when she had requested a half-dollar raise per week. The daughter, upon seeing a photograph of the girl, remembers that she was a shop assistant that she had complained about, in a fit of temper, to the manager. The girl was subsequently released from her job. The questions continue around the family circle until it becomes apparent that each member had some contact with the young girl. In all the cases the condemning evidence was there that each had helped drive Eva Smith into the despair of darkness where she took her life. As the play progresses, the police inspector looks less like an officer and more like God questioning his children about this unfortunate happening.

We are all often guilty of serving up complaints to those who serve in various capacities. Rather than lifting the dragging spirits of those who stand and serve, we so easily can put heavy weights on their heads by critical glances and comments. I have often wondered why nine out of ten lepers healed by Christ did not come back and give thanks. Maybe they would have responded, "Oh, did he expect us to? We thought it was his job to do things like that. We heard he was called the Good Physician. It never occurred to us that we should thank someone who was merely doing his duty." That attitude is very common; it circles the globe. Why thank someone to whom we pay the bills? Consequently, doctors, teachers, and clerks in stores are seldom thanked. Yet they all need more than money. They need the articulation of appreciation from those upon whom they wait.

Along with thinking that work done in the line of duty does not require our thanks, we also are slow with gratitude to those who seem to like what they are doing. After all, their personal satisfaction should be payment enough! If Mom goes around the house singing while she cooks, makes beds, and sews on buttons, many family members forget to give thanks because if Mom appears so happy she must be having fun doing these chores. How little they really know!

If the fabric of life is to hold together, we must all sew a stitch of gratitude into every act of service that is performed for us. Start today. The clerk at the store, the teacher in the classroom, the service station attendant should hear the punctuation of a "Thanks" at the end of their task for you. God hears it too.

Gratitude stimulates service to one another.

38 | Say it to friends

A friend loves at all times, and a brother is born for adversity (Prov. 17:17).

There are friends who pretend to be friends, but there is a friend who sticks closer than a brother (Prov. 18:24).

In the midst of a tragic accident in our family an old college classmate sent me a long letter. We have shared many good times together, and contact has been intact throughout the years. He wrote: "Our thoughts and prayers have constantly been with you and I only wish that in times like these that we lived a little closer so that we could make ourselves more useful. Friends are meant to be of help and all I can say is that we sure feel useless in a time like this." He went on to write words of comfort and compassion. But my friend was far from useless. His prayers and thoughts descended like dew on the parched soil of our souls.

A popular song from the musical *Funny Girl* suggests that people who need people are lucky. I agree. God did not make us for isolationism. Stevenson said, "No man is useless while he has a friend." Friends give meaning to your life, and also when you have friends, you have the compelling opportunity and necessity of giving yourself. Your friends can know all about you, and they still like you. Even when you make a fool of yourself, they don't feel that you've done a permanent job!

Albrecht Dürer was born in 1471 in Germany. His close friend was a young man whom we know only by the name of Hans. The two were struggling young artists who desperately tried to support themselves while they studied. The need to work kept them from many of their classes. One day Hans, the older of the two, proposed that Albrecht should devote all his time to study, and he would support them both by working at a trade. Dürer studied during the succeeding years and became one of the great painters of that day. Hans supported his friend with tough manual labor that left his hands gnarled, and his fingers too stiff to effectively wield a paintbrush again.

Albrecht Dürer, out of a heart overflowing with love and gratitude to Hans, immortalized his friend's hands on canvas. His *Praying Hands* tells the eloquent story of self-giving, and future generations are enriched by this masterpiece of art.

Cicero commented, "What sweetness is left in life, if you take away friendship? Robbing life of friendship is like robbing the world of the sun." Friendship is like salt on food; it makes life taste good.

Jesus said, "I have called you friends" (John 15: 15). The Bible says of Moses that the Lord spoke to him face to face, "as a man speaks to his friend" (Exod. 33:11). Abraham was called, according to James, "the friend of God" because he believed God and obeyed him (James 2:23).

> Oh, this world's a curious compound,
> With its honey and its gall,
> With bitter cares and crosses,
> But a good world after all.
> And a good God must ha' made it,
> Leastways, that's what I say
> When a hand's upon my shoulder
> In a friendly sort o' way.
>
> Author unknown

Being a friend is thanksliving.

39 | Say it to the talented

> *If one member is honored, all rejoice together* (1 Cor. 12:26).

A story of two traveling companions goes this way. One man was controlled by envy, and the other man was contaminated with greed. A stranger met them at a fork in the road and told them that he wanted to give them a gift. Only one wish would be granted. Whichever man asked first would receive that which he requested. The other man would then receive a double portion of the same. The greedy man knew what he wanted but could not stand the thought of his companion getting twice as much as he received. The man dominated by envy also knew what he desired but became "green in the face" when he thought of the other man having a double allotment. They both remained silent, stewing inside themselves. The stranger told them they had to make up their minds and record their request. Finally the man of greed took the man of envy by the throat and demanded that he make his wish known. The man of envy gasped, "I wish to be made blind in one eye." As soon as he said it, blindness covered his one eye. The greedy man then received double portion. He became blind in both eyes.

Because it is buried in the grave of greed and envy, much gratitude never grows in the garden of life. I read some history about the decorating of the grand hall in Florence, Italy. All the outstanding artists were asked to submit drawings. There seemed to be little doubt that Leonardo da Vinci would be the man for the job. But there was a young artist by the name of Michelangelo who submitted sketches that were most magnificent. The committee decided to give this young man the assignment. It is said that when the news of this selection was received by Leonardo da Vinci, the old artist went into a decline from which he never completely recovered.

It is a difficult thing to rejoice with those who attain greater achievement in the same endeavor in which you are competing. Our culture has bred a "got-to-win" personality that thinks everything is failure unless you stand on top of the heap of humanity. Envy envelops the individual who is a step or two behind the leader in brains, beauty, or bank account.

Our faith fortunately can free us from the strangulating effect of envy. We begin to see ourselves as a family, members one of another. So Paul exhorts the church at Corinth, "If one member is honored, all rejoice together." Dr. Harry Emerson Fosdick said, "The psychologically healthy person rejoices in the excellence of others. Objectively interested in whatever he is giving his life to, he is glad when a musician, teacher, or administrator appears who is better than himself." Goethe reminds us of the secret of such sentiment, "Against the superiority of another the only remedy is love."

Surely we must all give life our best effort. Then when someone passes us on the track, we don't give them a scowl but rather a smile. Because we are involved in humanity, we rejoice in records being broken in every realm. And we realize that, "Every good endowment and every perfect gift is from above, coming down from the Father of lights with whom there is no variation or shadow due to change (James 1:17).

Talents that top ours should be saluted with thanksgiving.

40 Say it to country

First of all, then, I urge that supplications, prayers, intercessions, and thanksgivings be made for all men, for kings and all who are in high positions, that we may lead a quiet and peaceful life, godly and respectful in every way (1 Tim. 2:1-2).

Let every person be subject to the governing authorities. For there is no authority except from God, and those that exist have been instituted by God. (Rom. 13:1).

Sir Walter Scott penned it: "Breathes there the man, with soul so dead, Who never to himself hath said, This is my own, my native land!"

A little girl took a trip to New York City with her father. They took a boat trip and saw the Statue of Liberty guarding the entrance to the Harbor. The girl was fascinated with the history of the grand lady of liberty. As they returned across the bay that evening, the daughter stood by the boat's railing and watched the lady who held the lighted torch recede in the distance.

That night the little girl tossed on her pillow. She sat up and her father asked her what was wrong. She said, "Daddy, I was thinking about that lady out there in the dark with nobody to help her hold up her lamp. Shouldn't we help her?"

Some people look at a country with the eyes of a critic and wonder what is worth saving. Others ride like barnacles on the ship of state, looking for a free ride, without ever helping to hoist the sails that enable progress. But thank the Lord there are those who feel indebted to their country for the freedom which, though fragile, still lives on. And they still desire to help Miss Liberty hold aloft her lamp to the world.

Have you ever looked at your house with a scrutinizing eye? If you do, you will find errors made by the carpenters. The room arrangement might be a bit unhandy. There may be a slight leak in the faucet. Many faulty things can be found. However, let your house catch fire, and as you see it being consumed by the flames, you see much more than the faults. You see your home, and you realize that even though there are some negative things about it, the good things far outweigh them.

How do you say thanks to God for your country? Is the Pledge of Allegiance to the flag sufficient? I am afraid not. Involvement is the answer. First we must all be willing to prune the diseased branches of injustice, chicanery, and deceit from the tree of our national life. Then we must preserve the solid ancient landmarks which our fathers established. I appreciate the words of Benjamin Franklin at the framing of the constitution. He was 81 years of age and he said,

> I have lived a long time and the longer I live the more convincing proofs I see of this truth, that God governs the affairs of men. If a sparrow cannot fall to the ground without his notice, is it probable than an empire can rise without his aid? We have been assured, sir, in the sacred writings, that "Except the Lord build the house, they labor in vain that build it." I firmly believe this; and I also believe that without his concurring aid we shall succeed in this political building not better than the builders of Babel.

Thus we work to preserve the government of the people, by the people, and for the people.

Next we must pray for forgiveness and healing for our land. Gratitude does not just watch history march by, it makes history!

The flower of freedom is cultivated by gratitude.